M000230111

EASY PREY

EASY PREY

The Fleecing of
America's Senior Citizens
. . . and How to Stop It

Senator William S. Cohen

MARLOWE & COMPANY
NEW YORK

Published by
Marlowe & Company
632 Broadway, Seventh Floor
New York NY 10012

Copyright © 1997 by William S. Cohen

All rights reserved. No part of this book may be reproduced in any form without written permission from the publishers, unless by reviewers who wish to quote brief passages.

Library of Congress Cataloging in Publication Data

Cohen, William S.
    Easy prey: The fleecing of America's senior citizens... and how to stop it /
William S. Cohen
        p.   cm.
    Includes bibliographical references and index.
    ISBN 1-56924-737-4. — ISBN 1-56924-736-6 (pbk.)
    1. Aged—Crimes against—United States. 2. Aged—Crimes against—United
States—Prevention. 3. Fraud—United States. 4. Swindlers and swindling—United
States.
    I. Title
    HV8250.4.A34C64 1997
    384. 16'3'08460973—dc21   97-7509
                                                      CIP

ISBN 1-56924-737-3
ISBN 1-56924-736-6 (paper)

Manufactured in the United States of America.

In memory of
Reuben "Ruby" Cohen (1909-1995),
who lived and died on his own terms,
providing an easy mark for no man.

ACKNOWLEGMENTS

It has been my great privilege during my years in the United States House of Representatives and the United States Senate to serve with three outstanding advocates for our senior citizens.

First and foremost, I remain indebted to the late Congressman Claude Pepper of Florida who served as the first chairman of the House Select Committee on Aging. Through his words and deeds, he destroyed many of the myths and stereotypical images that society held about the elderly. He reminded us that, "Life is like riding a bicycle; you don't fall off unless you stop pedaling." Congressman Pepper pedaled to the very end of his life.

Second, I wish to acknowledge and praise the former chairman of the Senate Special Committee on Aging, John Heinz of Pennsylvania. I had served with John on the House Aging Committee during our years together there before being elected to the Senate. He was tireless in his efforts to root out fraud and waste from the programs so vital to our seniors. Tragically, he was killed in an airplane disaster while on his way to convene a hearing in his home state involving fraudulent suppliers of durable medical equipment. He left us long before his contributions were fully credited and before his mission could be completed.

Finally, I owe a great deal to my friend from Arkansas, Senator David Pryor, who has been an indefatigable leader on issues affecting the quality of life for our seniors and protecting them from all forms of exploitation. David has decided to retire from the Senate, but the high standard of excellence that he has set throughout his career as a Congressman, Governor, and Senator will be remembered with great fondness and gratitude by those who were honored to serve with him and those who were so honorably served by him.

William S. Cohen

CONTENTS

EASY PREY

INTRODUCTION

A proverb points to the paradox that confronts each of us: "Man fools himself. He prays for a long life but fears old age." Indeed, most of us wish to extend our presence among family and friends on this bountiful and beautiful planet for endless days. And thanks to the miracles of modern medicine, science, and pharmaceuticals, in addition to nutritious diets and physical exercise programs, we enjoy longer, healthier, and more productive lives. Yet the fear remains—fear that our earning capacities will have diminished, that our savings will prove too meager, that we will be unable to live independently, that the costs of institutional living will be beyond our means, that we are unprepared for the physical and mental impairments we may be forced to confront.

Then, too, there is the profound fear of violent and property-related crime, as the elderly are frequent and vulnerable targets of society's criminal element. The FBI has released a report which reflects a 3 percent drop in serious crime in 1994. According to the report:

- Murder and rape decreased by 5 percent
- Robberies were down 6 percent
- Aggravated assaults dropped 2 percent
- Burglaries fell 5 percent
- Larceny-theft and arson both dropped 1 percent

This is good news. Yet these statistics provide little comfort to Americans of any age, and particularly not to the elderly. Although the incidence of violent crimes may have decreased somewhat, the overall level of crime remains unacceptably high. Moreover, while the number of violent crimes may have dropped, the violence itself has intensified significantly, including car-jacking, murders, and random, drive-by shootings. Equally disturbing is the fact that violent crimes are being committed by juveniles at ever younger ages, adolescents who hold no respect for their peers, their parents, and least of all their elders.

Perhaps an even greater cause for fear is the growing number of schemes that are specifically targeted at our senior citizens, who because of their fixed incomes, limited savings, and diminished earning capacities have little opportunity to recover from the loss of any of their assets or survive funding reductions in programs that serve them.

In addition to providing protection to the safety and general welfare of the American people, our leaders and legislators are called on to construct a social safety net to help insure that our final years are made as gentle and generous as possible. Among the most important elements of that safety net is the availability of a high quality and affordable health care system. Although there is much to be proud of—and enough to find fault with—in our present health care system, it is under constant attack by a multitude of brazen and unscrupulous predators who, driven by greed, exhibit no remorse or mercy while fleecing the most vulnerable and unwitting of our citizens.

The methods employed by these conmen (and conwomen) range

from the simple to the sophisticated, but the end result remains the same—the draining away of billions of dollars that could be used to lower the overall costs of health care to consumers or to cover the needs of the millions of Americans who find themselves and their families in need of health care coverage.

The trustees of the Medicare Trust Fund have advised the nation that unless action is taken to correct current trends, the Medicare Trust Fund that pays hospital bills will be bankrupt just about five short years from now. Obviously, an aging population when coupled with a smaller work force will place stress upon the solvency of the program. Under these circumstances, it becomes all the more imperative to prevent criminals from robbing the elderly, not only of their dreams, but of their necessities.

Scam artists do not confine their feeding habits to our nation's health care programs. They will filch lifetime savings and even homes while wearing the guise of a family banker or friendly handyman. Home repairs, prize giveaways, high-risk investments, living trusts, unneeded "free" (and dangerous) medical supplies—all are included in the black bag of tricks carried by white-collar criminals.

In the following pages, I will provide the examples of how shockingly simple it has been—and continues to be—to steal billions of dollars from programs designed to help senior citizens and relate the personal stories of some senior citizens who have been preyed upon by the heartless. It is my hope that we will learn much from the lessons and regrettable losses of others.

William S. Cohen
October 1995

CHAPTER ONE

The Thin Gray Line

When bad men combine, the good must associate; else they will fall one by one, an unpitied sacrifice in a contemptible struggle.

—*Edmund Burke*

It's a fact of life—we're all growing older. Not only as individuals, but as a nation. If it's true that numbers (particularly if they're counted correctly) don't lie, then we have some major challenges to confront as a society. Call them demographics or simply statistics. Either way, they add up to a daunting reality.

By the year 2030, the over 65 population will double and the number of persons over 85 will triple. During the next twenty-five years, the elderly population in the United States will expand from being 12 percent of the total population to 25 percent, and there will be fewer than three working persons for each person over the age of 65. In fact, in little more than three decades, our aging population will drive combined Medicare, Medicaid, and Social Security spending to approximately 14 percent of the entire economy.

All of which means that we can't waste a day or a dollar in taking action to shape our policies to insure that this expanding segment of our population will receive the care, dignity and security that it deserves.

Cicero, the great Roman orator, once observed that, "Old age is respectable so long as it asserts itself, maintains its rights, is subservient to no one, and retains its sway to the last breath." While the needs of our senior citizens are, and will continue to be, many, perhaps the most important area where the elderly must maintain their sway is in that of health care.

Congress responded to this need in 1965 when it created the Medicare Act in order to provide medical insurance coverage for all citizens who were 65 years or older. Medicaid, a program that is funded in part by the federal government and administered by the states, was adopted to provide for health care to the poor and disabled regardless of age. The mandate of both Medicare and Medicaid was simple enough: Make sure that the hospital and doctor bills—provided they were reasonable, of course—were paid. But simple to declare has not proven simple to do. In spite of the many and complex procedures that have been established to prevent liars and larcenists from robbing the public and private medical insurance programs that serve our seniors, we continue to lose billions of dollars every year.

It is appallingly easy to commit health care fraud. The size, complexity, and splintering of the current health care system creates an environment ripe for abuse.

Health care fraud is an equal opportunity employer that does not discriminate against any part of the system. All government health care programs—Medicare, Medicaid, CHAMPUS—and other federal and state health plans, as well as private sector health plans, are ravaged by fraud and abuse.

Similarly, no one type of health care provider group corners the market on health care fraud. Scams against the system run the gamut from small companies or practitioners who occasionally pad their Medicare billings to large criminal organizations that steal millions of dollars from Medicare, Medicaid, and other insurers. FBI Director Louis Freeh testified in Congress that health care fraud is growing much faster than law enforcement ever anticipated and that even cocaine distributors are switching from drug dealing to health care fraud schemes because the chances of being caught are so small—and the profits are so big. Fraud is systemic in the health care industries providing services to our nation's elderly and disabled Americans. The inspector general of the Department of Health and Human Services, for example, has cited problems in home health care, nursing home, and medical supplier industries as significant trends in Medicare and Medicaid frauds and abuses. Padding claims and cost reports, charging the government and patients outrageous prices for services, and billing Medicare for costs having nothing to do with patient care are just a few of the schemes perpetrated in these industries.

Unscrupulous providers are enjoying a feeding frenzy on Medicare and Medicaid, while taxpayers are picking up the tab for the feast.

A major step we can and must take toward Medicare and Medicaid reform is to crack down on the fraud and abuses that drive up the costs of health care for senior citizens and taxpayers. Estimates are that Medicare and Medicaid combined lose about $33 billion each year to fraud and abuse, and that losses in the entire health care system and our economy to fraud exceed $100 billion each year. If Willie Sutton were alive today, he wouldn't have to rob any banks. He'd simply tunnel his way into the health care system—because that's where the real money is.

Where are the police when you really need them? It's a fair question to ask. Aren't there laws, rules, regulations, high-powered computers, inspectors, FBI agents, federal prosecutors to protect us from the charlatans and cheats?

The answer is yes—and no. There are laws and regulations, but they are weak and riddled with loopholes large enough for battleships to sail through. And there can never be enough federal and state enforcement authorities to catch society's scavengers.

The FBI, for example, has only 249 agents assigned to conduct health care fraud investigations. The inspector general located in the Department of Health and Human Services assigns about 200 employees to health care fraud investigations. (It is hard to judge just how many actual people are assigned to investigations because the department measures this work by a bureaucractic term—full-time equivalent (FTE)—that covers 225 to 230 people.) More than four billion claims for federal and private health plans are processed annually. The mathematical matchup is redoubtable: The two predominant health care anti-fraud enforcement agencies have only the equivalent of one investigator per about 8,500,000 claims.

In 1994, the FBI was able to achieve 353 criminal convictions and retrieve some $480 million in fines, restitutions, and other recoveries. This sounds impressive only until we measure this amount against the $40 billion that is being siphoned off illegally just from the federally funded programs. But it is a sad reality that we face in virtually every aspect of law enforcement. Large amounts of money inevitably attract the attention of the criminally minded. This is especially the case when there is very little chance that they will be detected, apprehended, prosecuted, or if convicted, face lengthy confinement in prison

Nearly fifteen years ago, the Senate Special Committee on Aging, in assessing the lure of large and quick profits in the health care industry, turned not only to law enforcement officials, but to a "hands-on" expert—a physician from Philadelphia. He was an impressive witness with equally impressive credentials as a noted cardiologist. He was open and expansive, with a soft-spoken and gentle manner that invited trust and confidence. He was also a convicted felon who had defrauded both public and private health insurers in three states for more than $500,000 by submitting $1.5 million in claims for medical services he had never performed, and had spent some three years in prison.

Apparently subscribing to Oscar Wilde's witticism that he could resist everything but temptation, the doctor declared that the fault lay not in his heart, but in the not-so-starry system. "The problem," he said, "is that nobody is watching. Because of the nature of the system, I was able to do what I did. The system is extremely easy to evade. The forms I sent in were absolutely outrageous. I was astounded when some of the payments were made." The doctor arrived in Philadelphia carrying not only his medical school diplomas, but also a record of seven arrests and five convictions for fraud in New York, Connecticut, and Texas. Yet he was allowed to practice medicine in the state of Pennsylvania.

Clearly, neither he nor we learned very much from his life in the crime lane. His license to practice (and opportunity to steal) was reinstated by Pennsylvania authorities in 1990. In February of 1991, he opened a diagnostics and weight-loss practice in Philadelphia. He might still be wearing a white smock and a large smirk were it not for a former patient who, angry with his false billings, agreed to act as an undercover agent for federal officials.

This doctor has once again been convicted of filing false claims for millions of dollars for procedures never performed. Federal District Court Judge John P. Fullam, who sentenced this health care fraud expert, was completely bewildered. "What I have trouble understanding," he said before deciding the doctor's fate, "is was everybody asleep? With this record how could he be practicing medicine and sending in bills and still be getting paid?"

The doctor offered, in his defense, that he was a victim of an undiagnosed and untreated bipolar disorder (manic-depression). Judge Fullam was not impressed. He concluded that it was not mental illness but greed that motivated the doctor. On May 3, 1995, he sentenced "Dr. Fraud" to serve seventy-one months in prison without the possibility of parole and imposed a fine of $4 million.

This case illustrates how flawed the monitoring of our health care delivery system is and the important role that beneficiaries play in detecting and reporting suspicious or fraudulent activity. Given the budget realities of today and for the foreseeable future, we are not likely to see a geometric increase in the number of federal investigators and auditors. In fact, we will need to continue to rely upon the first line of defense against fraudulent conduct—the Medicare beneficiaries themselves. While they are in no position to know whether surgical procedures or medical devices are reasonably priced, at least they can say whether the medical services were actually rendered or the medical equipment even needed.

Many times, simple common sense or experience tells them that something is "rotten in Denmark"—or Denver,—and they, much like members of a neighborhood crime watch team, should call the police. But what happens if no one answers the phone, or if they're told they called the wrong station, or that it's only a petty crime, and, besides, why bother, because the property loss is covered by a national homeowners insurance policy?

Take the case of Otto Twitchell of Wyoming. In the summer of 1989, Otto's daughter was suffering from hepatitis and under a doctor's care. The family doctor advised all members of the Twitchell family to have a gamma globulin shot to protect them against the spread of the disease. Otto's wife, another daughter, son-in-law, and two granddaughters each received a shot at the doctor's office. The charge was $15 each. Another granddaughter went to the county health department and received her shot for $3.

Otto was fishing in a remote part of Wyoming when his wife sent him a letter advising him of the doctor's recommendation that he obtain a gamma globulin shot. He drove sixty-five miles to the town of Rock Springs and entered the hospital there for the sole purpose of receiving the shot. A doctor checked his blood pressure and then checked his chest using a stethoscope. After a nurse gave him the injection, she advised him to wait in the lobby for a few minutes to be sure he did not experience any ill effects such as an upset stomach.

Otto's only reaction to the shot came several weeks later when he received a summary of the charges that the hospital had billed to Medicare. He was shocked. The bill was $417. The statement indicated that he had been given Hepatitis B Immune Globulin instead of the gamma globulin recommended by his family physician.

Otto decided that the Medicare system was being "ripped off" and that everyone should be concerned because "it just contributes to the cost of the program for all of us." He was morally indignant and mad. But he had no idea of the obstacles and insults he would face in launching his protest.First, he called a Medicare tollfree number to complain, not only because it would have been a long-distance charge to call the hospital in Greenwater, but he knew the effort would prove futile. The Medicare operator, located in Washington, D.C., said that Wyoming was "out of their area" and could do nothing. This response puzzled Otto because he thought Medicare was a national program and a matter of concern to all geographic areas, including the nation's capital.

He then called his supplemental insurance carrier and was told that if Medicare had approved the bill, nothing could be done. His anger kept smoldering. He called another Medicare toll- free number, this one located in Denver, Colorado, and an operator asked him why he was creating such a fuss since the bill had been paid and no one was taking money out of his pocket!

Anger turned to bitterness. He was made to feel that he was guilty of wrongdoing for complaining. At his wife's suggestion, he called his congressman, whose assistant initially thought that the congressman could not be helpful because the hospital was not in his district. But after reviewing the extraordinary charge, the assistant had Otto sign a document authorizing the Congressman to investigate the matter.

Approximately a month later, the Denver regional office of the Department of Health and Human Services called Otto to inquire about his complaint. The representative badgered and insulted him, insinuating that he was the guilty party for wasting the government's time on such a trivial matter. Otto slammed the phone down on him. The system had been turned upside down. It was none of his business. Someone else was paying the bill. Never mind that he was that "someone else"—the American taxpayer!Otto was resigned to carrying his resentment and regret around like a stone in his shoe. Then four months later, he received a letter from the hospital indicating that it had made a mistake. The bill should have been $115. Otto's share of that cost was $16.85. He sent the check. Later, he received an apology from the Denver regional office for the treatment he had received from an operator who was trained to give the "pat" answers he had received. A retraining program would be instituted so that other citizens would not receive similar treatment when calling to report an overcharge.

Otto Twitchell's story is a classic example of the axiom that "no good deed goes unpunished." But if it were not for honest men and women like him, we would continue to solidify the mind-set that we are all entitled to something because someone else is paying the bill. It's a government-issued gold credit card that you can use and never have to pay for. It's the same mentality that accounts for why we are running up massive federal budget deficits and will, unless our spending habits change, pass on a debt of $5 trillion to our children and grandchildren.

The amount of money that Otto Twitchell contested may have been "trivial" in the mind of the federal employee who berated him, but a $400 injection here and there, to paraphrase the famed Illinois senator, Everett Dirksen, can add up to real money!

Another example of how a seemingly insignificant problem can burn a big hole in the taxpayer's pocket can be found in the case of an elderly woman who lives in a board and care home in Sanford, Maine. She fell one day and suffered a small cut in her forearm that was less than an inch long and not deep enough to require the attention or services of a physician.

An unscrupulous medical equipment supplier delivered packets of 6"x8" waterproof dressings. The woman used, at most, fourteen of these dressings at a total cost of less than $40. Actually, a trip to the local pharmacy by the manager of the boarding home would have saved the taxpayer $25 or more, but let's not quibble over a few stacks of pennies.

Perhaps it was simply a computer error or that the supplier believed that the woman's wound was running like the Red Sea. But the company billed Medicare $850 for fifty of these dressings. Additional packets of dressings were delivered. There were boxes of them, along with enough tubes of anti-septic gels to service a small war zone. The total bill submitted to Medicare: $3,510!

A supply company in California was even more brazen. It billed Medicare $5 million for post-surgery dressings for nursing home patients who had never undergone surgery. Apparently, Medicare reimbursed several nursing homes in different states for the dressings and the homes, in turn, paid a percentage to the supply company.

While the general elderly population serves as a target for scam artists, the most vulnerable are those who are poor, who do not speak or read English well, if at all, who subsist on Social Security Supplemental Income (SSI) and other government-supported programs, and who do not have family members living nearby who can help protect them from scavengers or become their advocates when they have been victimized.

South Florida offers a prime example of how some of our most vulnerable seniors are being exploited. In the Dade County community known as "Little Havana," many of the elderly residents speak Spanish only. One woman went to a person to have her toenails cut. A little while later she received a statement from Medicare that an orthopedist had billed Medicare for over $2,000 for services rendered.

Another woman who lived to the age of 103 had been receiving physical therapy. Months after she had died, her niece received Medicare statements indicating that her aunt was still receiving physical therapy. Now most of us hope and believe that there is life after death—but physical therapy too?

In a housing unit for seniors, a woman was given a document that was printed in both English and Spanish. It was an application to join a "Medicare-Medicaid Club." The applicants who signed the form were promised cash, free groceries, specially made orthotic shoes, and free transportation. Of course, one of the blanks to be filled in was the applicant's Medicare number. Upon receipt of the application form, the operators of the "club" proceeded to bill Medicare for goods and services that were not medically needed, and, of course, not delivered.

Mrs. Victoria Torres was at a food stamp office when she was approached by another woman who claimed to be working for the government. The woman inquired whether Mrs. Torres was experiencing any stomach problems. When Mrs. Torres replied in the affirmative, the woman advised her that the government was supplying "free milk," a nutrition formula called Sistocal, that would help her with her digestive problems. Mrs. Torres, believing the woman to be a government employee, completed a prepared form and provided the woman with her Medicare card.

Within a matter of days, a man driving a white, unmarked van delivered the "free milk" to Mrs. Torres' home. The thick and sweet liquid certainly was not milk, and, after a few sips, Mrs. Torres decided she could not drink it. Subsequently, Medicare sent Mrs. Torres a statement that it had paid a claim in the amount of $737 for five cases of formula and thirty-one supply kits. When Mrs. Torres' daughter discovered what had happened, she contacted a Medicare office immediately to relate the problem and demand that Medicare investigate the matter. She also wrote a letter requesting that she be given copies of all statements for which Medicare had been billed for the Sistocal that was supplied to her mother.

Mrs. Torres' daughter was shocked to discover that Medicare had been billed $7,000 for fifty cases of Sistocal along with feeding kits and equipment! She wrote Medicare once again to complain. Her reward was the receipt of a copy of the statement that her mother had originally received in the amount of $737. Again she protested. Medicare advised Mrs. Torres to stop accepting any deliveries of Sistocal. Mrs. Torres did precisely that, refusing to accept or sign for any further deliveries. But Medicare continued to be billed for more deliveries to Mrs. Torres—even in the two months following a major hurricane which had completely destroyed her home. The total bill for the unneeded "free milk"—$7,930.

Ms. Sharon Rager of West Palm Beach stumbled upon the practice on the part of at least one nursing home of providing unnecessary psychiatric services to its residents. Ms. Rager's grandmother, who had suffered a number of severe shocks, has poor vision, is extremely hard of hearing, and frequently does not recognize family members who visit her in the nursing home. One day she discovered that a psychiatrist visited the nursing home and dropped by to say hello to her grandmother. The charge to Medicare? $125.

It's important to note that Ms. Rager's grandmother, who is not mentally ill, would not know who the psychiatrist was or what he was saying to her unless he were shouting directly into her ear. Even then, according to Ms. Rager, her grandmother would have no memory of the conversation two minutes after the psychiatrist had departed. Not only would the psychiatrist send one of his associates over to the nursing home in his place, but all of the residents of the home would be gathered into the activities room for a group session at a charge of $55 per resident. None of the residents could understand the conversation, if indeed, they ever heard it.

When Ms. Rager's mother received a statement from Medicare revealing the charges, she immediately complained to the nurses at the home and demanded that they stop providing the psychiatric services. The services would stop for one month and then be reinstituted. Finally, after repeated complaints, the psychiatric visits were terminated, but only for the grandmother, not for all of the other residents. The cost charged to Medicare for unnecessary, unwanted services to this one resident totaled $950.

As Ms. Rager has said, "Everyone is crying about health care waste, but we all continue to look the other way or take advantage ourselves. I feel if I do not speak up I will be as guilty as the psychiatrist. It has to stop. We can no longer let apathy and greed rob our government."

———

Federal officials continue to maintain that Medicare and Medicaid beneficiaries provide the front line of defense against fraudulent and abusive conduct. If this is the case, we need to ask exactly how easy do we make it for them to carry out this responsibility? The answer is—not very.

After beneficiaries have received medical treatment or equipment, Medicare sends a statement listing the charges that have been billed to and paid by Medicare. It's called an Explanation of Medical Benefits (EOMB). Even an expert in Egyptian hieroglyphics might have difficulty deciphering a physician's bill and what Medicare will pay. But when conscientious beneficiaries detect a glaring error— such as when Medicare is billed for three X rays or pieces of equipment when only one was received—they may feel as if they have been stranded on a sandbar somewhere in the Pacific and reduced to stuffing an S.O.S. message in a bottle and casting it adrift, praying that some soul will find it and come to their rescue.

Consider the case of Eleanor Lankay, an elderly woman from Union, New Jersey, who suffered from arthritis . In the Spring of 1989, a woman called her on the telephone and advised her that she was entitled to a multitude of medical equipment and supplies for free.

Mrs. Lankay declined the offer. The caller then asked if she suffered from arthritis. When Mrs. Lankay confirmed that she did, the woman requested and was given the name of her physician. Within several days, a package containing a paraffin wax bath and heating pad was delivered by UPS to Mrs. Lankay's home. Fortunately, she was never tempted to use the wax bath to determine if it would, as represented, alleviate her arthritis. The person who had contacted her by phone to obtain her physician's name never offered to provide instruction for the item's use or alert her to any dangers from using the product.

Included in the box were certain warnings, such as, "Caution, this surface may be hot." The label on the wax itself stated, in print that would prove challenging to anyone with less than perfect vision: "The wax pan refill is to be used only in a Thermane bath heating appliance. Paraffin wax can ignite, causing serious injury to your person and property. Do not heat on stove, burner, hot plate, or any open flame. Scalding and burning can result from improper use." Somewhere in the written materials was a notice that the wax could reach temperatures up to 136 degrees, but there were no instructions as to the prudent length of time the user should submerge an extremity in the wax in order to avoid scalding and burning.

Initially, Mrs. Lankay asked her doctor about the equipment and he stated that he knew nothing about it. She placed an 800 number telephone call to the company that had sent the package and requested that they send someone to pick up the equipment. No one ever came.

A short time thereafter, Mrs. Lankay began to receive papers from Medicare which indicated that the supplier of the equipment used the name National Royal Corporation. She called Medicare, related her story, and requested the stopping of all payments (which were averaging more than $60 a month) for equipment that she neither asked for nor wanted.

The Medicare operator advised her that it was impossible to stop such payments and that Mrs. Lankay should call the home care company to request them to retrieve the equipment that she considered worthless. Mrs. Lankay called the number furnished to her and, much to her surprise, reached a number in a restaurant in Plainfield, New Jersey, where only Spanish was spoken. She then tried calling the original number she had called, only to have an operator tell her that the 800 number had been canceled and that no further information was available.

Mrs. Lankay turned for help to a man named Sam Vitale, a retiree who was serving as a SHIP (Senior Health Insurance Program) counselor. It was his job to assist seniors work their way through the complex maze associated with Medicare claims. After reviewing the facts of her case, Mr. Vitale confronted Mrs. Lankay's physician, who again professed ignorance about the matter. The doctor suggested that Mr. Vitale contact the local county medical society.

Now Mr. Vitale, a man with four years of experience in dealing with these issues, began to share Mrs. Lankay's frustration. He called Medicare, the Health Care Financing Administration (HCFA), Social Security, and the local medical society—and each time was met with either indifference or incompetence.

He found Medicare's hot line to be particularly useless. The hot line respondent referred him to the New Jersey Health Department. The Health Department declared that it was not its problem and suggested that he try another 800 number, that of New Jersey's Consumer Complaint Division, which, of course, had no jurisdiction over health care. He thought he had arrived at a dead end.

As a last resort, Mr. Vitale returned to Mrs. Lankay's physician, who, upon further research into his files, discovered that he had signed a Certificate of Medical Necessity which had authorized Federal Health Care to furnish Mrs. Lankay with the paraffin hot wax bath. Mr. Vitale thought it unusual that the Certificate contained a two-year authorization instead of the customary shorter period of time that allows the physician to conduct a follow-up examination to determine whether further treatment is necessary. He gathered all the information and presented it to a number of sources, including Medicare authorities.

Mrs. Lankay's and Mr. Vitale's persistence was rewarded later that year. The Department of Health and Human Services filed a civil fraud complaint against two durable medical equipment suppliers and nine individual defendants. The suit stated that the home care company "contacted Medicare beneficiaries by telephone, obtained their Social Security numbers, prepared false medical certificates concerning Medicare beneficiaries' conditions, induced the patients' physicians to execute false certificates, and shipped unneeded and unwanted medical equipment to the beneficiaries." Medicare had been billed over $8 million during a two-year period and had made payments of more than $4 million.

If the federal government expects Medicare (and Medicaid) beneficiaries to serve as the first alert to fraud and abuse, then it needs to make the complaint system more "user friendly," starting with training hot line operators to respond positively to complaints rather than treating them as the problem. The overwhelming majority of complaints involve either clerical errors or misunderstandings. But when red flags are raised and clearly visible, then the complaints should be vigorously pursued. And, besides discouraging citizens who report questionable billings or practices, the government has actually contributed to the dissemination of erroneous information to Medicare patients on how much they owe.

This is how the system should work: Medicare pays 80 percent of the amount it considers "reasonable" for physician and other outpatient services. The Medicare patient is then responsible for the remaining 20 percent of the "reasonable" charges. Most Medicare claims are filed by physicians who accept this arrangement which in effect, sets a limit on their fee for providing service. But about 20 percent of doctors do not accept the Medicare "reasonable" amount, and bill Medicare patients above and beyond the Medicare allowable amount.

In 1989, Congress passed legislation limiting the amount that physicians could charge patients over that allowed by Medicare, in order to prevent Medicare patients from being hit with huge out-of-pocket expenses. As of 1993, the amount that a physician could charge a beneficiary was limited to 115 percent of the fee considered to be "reasonable" by Medicare. This limit was obviously intended to protect the 34 million Medicare beneficiaries from excessive out-of-pocket expenses which were proving ruinous for most of them. But the Health Care Financing Administration (HCFA), which administers Medicare, was lax and careless about enforcing the limits, spotting the abusers, and informing citizens about their rights to challenge physicians who overcharged. In fact, Medicare routinely mailed out obsolete and erroneous explanation of benefit forms, misleading beneficiaries into believing that they owed far more than the law allowed.

This misleading information added up to real money for some senior citizens. In one case, for example, a New York doctor charged a woman $4,063 for the surgery he had performed. By law, the charges were supposed to be limited to a maximum of $1,072. Medicare did not spot the error and proceeded to notify the patient that she was responsible for paying $3,335! Sadly, this was not an isolated or unique situation. Rather, senior citizens across the country were informed by Medicare that they had to pay excessive amounts charged by their doctors—even though the law was on their side. Worse, there was no requirement for the doctor to refund a patient's overpayment if the doctor exceeded the billing limits. Thus, the Medicare beneficiary was not only stripped of the law's protection but also left without any means of obtaining restitution of the money that was never owed in the first place. The problem was of a sufficient magnitude to prompt a number of groups to initiate legal proceedings against the federal government to enforce the billing limits.

Many of the physicians who submitted claims in excess of what was allowed did so through inadvertence or ignorance of the law's new limits. Greed may have motivated others. But there can be no excuse for the guardians of the system failing to enforce the law aggressively so that Medicare beneficiaries are not overcharged and then terrorized by a faceless, computerized bureaucracy that commands them to pay an obligation not owed.

The law, if it ever was ambiguous, has been clarified. It is now illegal for physicians to charge Medicare beneficiaries more than 115 percent over that amount determined by Medicare to be reasonable for Part B services. So, for example, if Medicare determines that $100 is a reasonable charge for a given service, it will pay the doctor 80 percent, or $80 in this case. Ordinarily, the beneficiary would pay the balance of $20. But a physician may believe that his service is worth $150 or even $200. By law, he can charge a maximum of $115. Therefore, at most the beneficiary would be liable for a total of $35. If any over payment is made, the physician is required to reimburse the beneficiary. In order to further protect Medicare patients, physicians who demonstrate a knowing and willful disregard for the law are subject to penalty.

Dos and Don'ts

- Telemarketing is a fancy name for doing business over the phone. Don't be intimidated. If you receive a solicitation over the phone, ask the caller to send all the materials by mail.

- Do not give your Social Security number, your Medicare, Medicaid, or health plan identification number—or the name of your physician—to any caller.

- Do not be fooled by the names "federal" or "national" that so many organizations frequently use to give the impression that they are government sponsored.

- Do not use equipment obtained by mail without professional instructions on how to use it safely.

- When you receive the Explanation of Medical Benefits (EOMB), look for charges that seem excessive or for services or goods never provided. A sample explanation of benefits form with a guide on how to read this form is included in the Appendix TK, page TK.

- Be sure to compare physician charges that you are responsible for under Part B of Medicare with the amount that Medicare has determined to be a reasonable fee.

- If you fail to receive prompt, courteous assistance when dealing with any federal agency representatives, contact your congressional representative or senator. Remember, these officials work for you and are paid by you.

- When you detect a questionable charge, call the insurance carrier that is acting on behalf of Medicare or call a Medicare hot line directly. Many Medicare carriers have established toll-free numbers for you to call and report suspected fraud and abuse. Do not be afraid to question the authority or accuracy of the billing. If your doctor's office is merely careless in its billing procedures, it should be grateful for your help in correcting poor performance. If your doctor or someone in his or her office is corrupt, then you will be helping to rescue our health care system from fraud. Since Medicare Part A is in danger of becoming insolvent by the year 2002 due to an enormous growth in health care costs, it is vital to rid Medicare of fraud and abuse that siphon off scarce federal dollars. Fear of reporting fraud will only hasten Medicare's fiscal demise.

CHAPTER TWO

Your Money and Your Life

Deceivers are the most dangerous members of society. They trifle with the best affections of our nature and violate the most sacred obligations.

—George Crabbe

There are over 160,000 suppliers of durable medical equipment (DME) doing business in the United States. The overwhelming majority of DME suppliers are legitimate business men and women who provide essential equipment, such as wheelchairs, hospital beds, oxygen supplies, and walking aids to the elderly or disabled. Tom Deschaine, for example, who lives in northern Maine, has worked in the health care field for more than twenty years and now operates a medical equipment supply business. Like most medical equipment suppliers, he does not solicit business over the phone and he makes extraordinary efforts to ensure that his customers are well served.

For one customer who required oxygen equipment, Mr. Deschaine traveled forty miles to deliver a two-and-a-half hour training session for the patient's friends and family. He made followup visits twice in one week, along with communicating by telephone to make sure that the equipment was functioning and that the customer was operating it properly. Regrettably, as we saw in the case of Mrs. Eleanor

Lankay's paraffin hot wax bath, not all DME suppliers have the best interests of the Medicare beneficiaries in mind. In fact, over the past several years, the DME industry has been cited by Congress and law enforcement officials as a major source of fraudulent and abusive activity.

DME providers are not required to be certified or licensed. Until very recently, they have not had to meet standards of any kind. An individual, or group of individuals, would simply secure one or more provider numbers and set up a business address which might be no more than a P.O. Box number. They would then undertake to provide medical equipment to Medicare and Medicaid beneficiaries and seek payment through the insurance carrier that provided the most generous reimbursement policies.

Frequently, these DME suppliers establish "telephone boiler rooms," utilizing teenagers and others with no medical background to make call after call to senior citizens to interest them in what they describe as "free medical equipment" to which they are entitled under the law. If a Medicare beneficiary yields to their importuning and indicates that he or she would like the equipment, the marketer sends an official-looking form to the recipient's physician for authorization.

Durable medical equipment is reimbursable by Medicare and Medicaid only if it is prescribed by physicians as being medically necessary. Usually, the doctors either are too busy to review the specific request on a Certificate of Medical Necessity (CMN) or wish to avoid agitating their patients who may be convinced that the item is needed—and free. Occasionally, the doctor might even act in complicity with the fraudulent supplier. In more than a few instances, the supplier bypasses the physician altogether and simply forges his signature on the CMN.

Once the CMN is in hand, the telemarketer sends out the equipment, even though it often is medically unnecessary, has no therapeutic benefit, and may even be dangerous because these salesmen do not take the same care with their customers as do legitimate dealers. The telemarketer then sends the doctor's CMN to Medicare, which pays 80 percent of the bill. The dealer is required by law to collect the remaining 20 percent from the recipient but rarely does so since the profit is quite handsome without it.

One DME telemarketer in Pennsylvania paid $28 for a piece of foam the size of a seat cushion. The Medicare carrier was billed for a wheelchair "flotation pad" and wrote a check for over $240.

In New York, a telemarketer paid $28.57 for a bed-size piece of pink foam, described it as a "dry flotation mattress," and billed Medicare for more than $1,100. A tidy profit of more than 3800 percent!

Orthotic body jacket scams have become increasingly popular. These custom-fit jackets are used by patients who have suffered back injuries or have undergone spinal surgery. Properly constructed, some of the jackets cost approximately $100 to manufacture, while Medicare pays roughly $800 for the item. Until 1990, the claims paid by Medicare for these jackets remained relatively stable. But over a two-year period, the number of claims soared from 275 to 17,910—an increase of 6400 percent. The cost to Medicare rose from $217,000 in 1990 to $18 million in 1992.

What Medicare sees on the CMN form is not always (and often never) what the beneficiary gets. One DME supplier in Texas defrauded Medicare of more than $1 million by billing Medicare for "body jackets," when he actually had provided wheelchair pads. The pads cost $50 to $100 to manufacture. The charge to Medicare? $1,300 per pad, an outrageous mark-up of 2500 percent.

Other scam artists supply a thin piece of plastic that wraps around one's back and is tied together in the front with two bands of wide string. The cost to manufacture these items charitably can be put at $15 to $19 and they would cost between $30 to $50 in a supply catalog. These have been billed to Medicare as "custom fit orthotic body jackets" for $520 each—a markup of as much as 1600 percent over the catalog price.

Wheelchair pads made of simple foam and vinyl have been marketed to nursing homes to hold residents in their wheelchairs—and then billed to Medicare, once again as the ever- popular body jacket at an average price of $930 each.

Other practices of disreputable DME suppliers include "unbundling" and "upcoding." Unbundling is the practice of submitting bills for the individual parts of a product at prices that far exceed the cost of the product as a whole. Upcoding involves the act of submitting bills for reimbursement using a payment code that represents a higher quality service or product than that actually provided, thereby resulting in a higher reimbursement to the provider.

An example of unbundling can be found in the sale of glucose monitoring kits used by diabetics daily to test their blood sugar. A perusal of virtually any newspaper advertisement would reveal that these kits can be purchased from a local drug store for approximately $40—or even as little as $10 or $12 after a manufacturer's rebate. In one case currently under investigation, Medicare was billed $250 for each kit, a 500 percent markup over the pharmacy retail price. The supplier defrauded Medicare by "unbundling" the kit and charging separately for each item—the monitor, lancets, lance holder, solution, and test strips. The supplier over-billed Medicare by unbundling, by double billing, and even billing for selling to patients who had already died.

A Pennsylvania DME company charged Medicaid for wheelchairs, particularly motorized ones, that had been unbundled, billing for separate items that are generally provided as standard equipment. The same company billed Medicaid for "incontinence liners" when, in fact, it had provided residents of a youth home and elderly nuns in a convalescent home with disposable washcloths.

A variation on the theme of upcoding involves ambulance and taxi service companies. In most states, Medicaid pays for a patient's transportation to a medical provider, either when mass transit is unavailable or when a patient's debilitating physical or mental condition precludes public transportation. A common practice on the part of some transport services is to overstate the miles traveled to the provider. Some clinics have billed for ambulance services when the transportation was provided by taxicabs, limousines, or shuttle buses.

A retired New York City police detective and two others were recently charged with stealing more than $442,000 from Medicaid between January 1989 and December 1994. The Long Island company was accused of making more than 9,000 fraudulent claims—including billing Medicaid for transporting six people who were dead at the time they were supposedly being transported.

Medical laboratories have also come under scrutiny for their flagrant abuse of the health care system. According to FBI Director Louis Freeh, a number of labs conduct a "sink test" during which samples of blood and urine are simply dumped down a drain by lab personnel who have performed no tests and then report that the test results are normal .

Other labs have increased their billings to the government and private health insurers by adding tests to their automated blood chemistry panel, referred to as SMAC (Sequential Multi-Analysis Computer). The series of tests is relatively inexpensive and provides valuable information to physicians and therefore is ordered almost routinely. These labs market the standard series as including a bonus of additional tests as a part of a health survey profile. Doctors are thereby misled into ordering the entire profile.

When the laboratories bill the government, private insurers, or patients, the extra tests are charged separately at much higher rates. This may sound like a rather insignificant scheme, but one company over a two-year period was able to increase its revenues from Medicare from less than $500,000 to $31 million by adding to its profile Ferritin, a test that measures iron in the blood.

In late 1994, a Maryland company was convicted of numerous

counts of fraud and theft. The lab performed diagnostic testing for many physicians in the greater Baltimore area. The defendants were charged with billing the government and private insurers for performing more than 8,000 unauthorized and useless tests that totaled nearly $150,000. The doctors either failed to notice the additional tests or assumed that they were performed automatically by technologically advanced equipment. Since the lab submitted the bills directly to the insurers, it was impossible for the physicians to know that huge extra costs had been added to the profiles.

Using the names of dozens of dead patients, a phantom laboratory in Miami allegedly cheated the government out of $300,000 in Medicare payments in a matter of weeks for tests that were never performed. The "lab" that submitted the bills consisted of a rented mailbox and a Medicare billing number.

The physician-owners of a clinic in New York stole over $1.3 million from Medicaid by billing for more than 50,000 "phantom" psychotherapy sessions never given to patients. In another New York case a psychiatrist pleaded guilty to cheating the state out of nearly half of the $850,000 paid her by the State Medicaid Program. She often billed for more than twenty-four hours of psychotherapy treatment in a single day!

A Detroit physician faces charges of Medicare, Medicaid, and private insurance fraud for filing claims for multiple services that were never provided to patients. The falsified services included claims for X rays, urinalysis, blood tests, and echocardiography. A New York physician was sentenced to two to six years in prison for charging the state for more than 25,000 methadone treatments he never gave. In his scheme he not only used the names of patients who had died but also patients whose names he randomly filched from hospital records.

In 1994, a Washington physician pleaded guilty to making false statements to the Medicaid program. He had others collect Medicaid identification cards from Cambodian residents during the period of

1991 to 1993. Upon delivery, the physician would write out pre-scriptions for the individuals named on the cards for medications that had been requested for them. He then filled out prescriptions for every family member listed on the cards even though they had not requested and did not need the medications. An intermediary would then receive $20 to $30 from the pharmacy to which the prescriptions were taken. The physician then fraudulently billed for two visits per month for every eligible Medicaid recipient for whom he had a card.

In Los Angeles, several individuals have been prosecuted for a $40 million fraudulent durable medical equipment scheme. Several DME companies were formed to bill Medicare and Medicaid for incontinence supplies that were either medically unnecessary or never delivered. The case also includes related civil litigation involving $3.5 million in foreign assets seized as far away as Liechtenstein.

A woman with a long career in health care started a company that supposedly conducted "lost charge audits." She began by going to a nursing home in the Seattle area and offering to increase revenue. She knew that the nursing home had not billed for bandages and dressings because they were considered routine costs included in the daily rate paid to the home by Medicare. Such a home rarely had need for surgical dressings because few patients have surgery in the home. But she put in claims for the dressings, buying 4" x 4" gauze pads costing less than a penny each when bought in bulk, and charging Medicare $5.60 to $7 for each dressing.

Within two months the nursing home was paid some $600,000 by Medicare for her false claims. She next worked the scheme at a San Francisco nursing home, where she succeeded in stealing another $600,000 from Medicare. "Every nursing home with which we dealt gleefully took the money and told other nursing home administrators of our service," she recalls. By the time she was caught, convicted, and jailed for fraud, she had conducted "lost charge audits" for at least seventy nursing homes in nine states. "It is easier than you can imagine to prepare false claims and have them paid by Medicare," she says.

Picking up on this theme, a former California nightclub owner said it was easy for him to cheat Medicare of $5.6 million in seventeen months. And he managed to do this a little over a year after serving a prison sentence on a drug charge. With a nurse he met in his nightclub, he set up a company and got a home health care license and Medicare certification from the Los Angeles County Department of Health Services.

The nurse quit the business after her partner began taking kickbacks from a physician who supplied patients' names, insurance numbers, and diagnostic codes. At the suggestion of Medicare officials, the nightclub owner turned health care provider began to send in claims electronically—a system that did not require any paperwork. He was soon billing Medicare for fake patients, including some who had not been seen by a physician for more than five years and some who were dead.

When Medicare/Blue Cross finally asked for some medical records, he paid nurses to write up notes and create fraudulent medical records. "We did talk to some nice ladies at Blue Cross who questioned why we were billing Medicare for home health services given to dead people," he recalls. "But we just told them we made a mistake and we were not paid for most of these claims."

In the seventeen months this one cheating company existed, it submitted more than 9,000 claims for more than 80,000 home health visits to 680 different patients. "We were paid $5.6 million, and between $1.5 and $2.5 million of that was for the fraudulent claims we sent in electronically during the last eight months of our operation," the owner says.

Medicare presented this man with a $2.5 million custom-built house in Bel Air, for which he paid a $1.2 million down payment. He also leased a Rolls Royce and a 500 SL Mercedes Benz. He pleaded guilty to five counts of mail fraud and conspiracy and is awaiting sentencing.

—

Most of us can remember the skit that comedian Jack Benny used to perform. He would relate to his audience the story of how he was accosted by a bandit who stuck a gun in his back and demanded, "Your money or your life!" Benny would then cast his soulful, dead-pan stare at the audience, lifting a forefinger to his cheek, pausing for seconds that seemed to stretch into minutes. Finally, he would reply to his agitated, gun-toting accoster, "Wait a minute, I'm thinking, I'm thinking." The audience usually howled with laughter at Benny's self-mocking reputation for frugality.

Laboratories that do "sink tests" are not only robbing federal and private coffers of millions of dollars. They are also endangering the lives of patients who have placed their trust—and lives—in them. Laboratory tests are often crucial in detecting early stages of serious and life-threatening diseases. A failure to make a proper analysis can mislead the doctor who, in turn, may fail to properly treat the patient. False positive readings have had tragic consequences in many cases. Phony tests or defective medical equipment can prove fatal.

Nowhere is this more graphically illustrated than in the case of a former pharmaceutical salesman who was the owner of a company which distributed human heart cardiac pulse generators and pulse generator leads. He was convicted of altering and misbranding expired pacemaker boxes to make them appear new. According to his former employees, he often acquired low-cost older models that were about to expire and re-labeled them. This meant that he not only was implanting pacemakers with old batteries but also was jeopardizing the devices' sterility and putting the patient at risk of infection.

When authorities raided the owner's office, they found a number of bloody pacemakers, raising suspicions that he was reselling devices that had been surgically removed from other patients or possibly corpses. One former employee said that she witnessed him washing off a pacemaker battery with tap water. In addition to distributing devices with lapsed expiration dates and recycling pacemakers that had not been properly sterilized, he also sent into the medical marketplace mislabeled pacemakers that were intended for "animal use only."

According to one of the investigators in this case, a retired electrician from Chicago was the unwitting beneficiary of one of the "mystery pacemakers" that had been implanted in his chest. No determination could be made of the brand, serial number, or expiration date of the pacemaker or the lead attached to his heart. The patient had absolutely no idea that the pacemaker was subject to failure or that he might have to undergo replacement surgery with all of the attendant risks.

What could possibly have prompted a physician to act like a dishonest mechanic who sticks a used carburetor under the hood of your car and charges you for a brand-new one? In a fundamental corruption of the Hippocratic oath, some of the physicians were given entertainment tickets, vacation trips to Hawaii, office medical equipment, cash, and the services of prostitutes in exchange for using the devices.

Unlike Jack Benny's moral dilemma, this isn't a question of "your money or your life." It's both.

Dos and Don'ts

- Deal only with established health care companies. If in doubt, get information from community or state agencies. (See Appendix 2.)

- If you suspect fraud, get in touch with one of these agencies. Do your part to kick fraudulent providers out of the Medicare and Medicaid programs so that they do not continue to rip off the system.

- Beware of telemarketers offering "free medical equipment." Durable medical equipment is reimbursable by Medicare and Medicaid only if a physician deems it to be medically necessary.

- If you or someone you know is receiving home care through a home health agency, get as much information as possible about the health providers. Find out, for example, whether licenses are required of those providers—and see that they have licenses.

- Laboratories bill the Medicare program directly and beneficiaries are not liable for any cost-sharing. But try to keep track of laboratory reports. Make sure that they are exactly what the doctor ordered. If you suspect irregularities, check with community or state agencies listed in Appendix 8.

CHAPTER THREE

The Tin Men

There's a sucker born every minute.

—*Phineas T. Barnum*

In 1987, we were treated to The Tin Men, a movie that starred actors Danny DeVito and Richard Dreyfuss. A witty satire, set in the early 1960s in the city of Baltimore, Maryland, it depicted the competitive hustle and private humiliations of two aluminum siding salesmen who sold the siding "free" but charged a $2,700 labor fee to gullible homeowners. DeVito and Dreyfuss represented a diminishing breed of shysters, who, not quite a half a step ahead of newly adopted consumer protection laws, see their status symbol, fin-tailed Cadillacs, go careening out of control along with their careers.

While federal and state consumer protection laws have had some impact on the free-wheeling, "separate-the-suckers-from-their-money" of conmen, those on the lower rungs of the evolutionary ladder have managed not only to survive but to flourish—particularly in the home-repair business. Omitted from the vocabulary of "hit and run" home-repair contractors are the words "shame" or "conscience." The only god they pray to is Mammon, who rewards them with the life savings of the innocent and unsuspecting. While no age group is considered off-limits to their scams, the elderly have become their prime targets of opportunity, principally because they usually have built up sizable equity in their homes, they are in greater need of assistance in repair work, and are either more trusting or more easily intimidated by their high-pressure sales tactics.

Most home-repair scams begin with a phone call. The Federal Trade Commission estimates that fraudulent telemarketing cheats U.S. consumers out of more than $1 billion each year. "Most telemarketers represent honest, reputable businesses," the FTC points out in a telemarketing warning pamphlet. "But because so many customers enjoy the ease and convenience of shopping by phone, it is an attractive tool for unscrupulous salesmen."

Attractive indeed! Cheating telemarketers know that their crimes are not easily traced and prosecuted. Working out of "boiler rooms"—rented space full of phones and fast-talking scam artists—they can move out of town quickly, then set up, probably under a new name, in another town.

Despite the problems of tracking them down and proving their crimes, the Federal Trade Commission, state attorney generals, and other watchdogs have closed down telemarketing scams that raked in more than $780 million. And in two recent years state investigators have cracked down on some 150 operators.

Spring and summer months seem to be the most lucrative time for the tin men to gather their rosebuds. A harsh winter may crack driveways and damage roofs or moldings. The clapboards may need painting, the yard fresh landscaping. With relentless singularity of purpose, the tin men focus on the vulnerabilities of their chosen victims and proceed to weaken their resistance with flattery, false promises, or intimidation. One fleece artist warned an elderly Chicago woman that her bungalow "had cancer of the bricks." It's unclear whether she believed that the cancer would consume her entire home, but she depleted her life savings in the vain effort to stop a non-existent disease.

Another repair man persuaded a 75-year-old woman that her sewer line had to be dug up because he detected the "smell" of radon gas in the basement. Radon, of course, is odorless.

Frequently, these contractors will persuade a homeowner to pay the full sum stated in the contract in advance and then abscond without delivering any service. There is a growing practice of persuading home owners to sign a written contract along with a blank loan application which is secured by a lien against the property. Often the work is shoddy and unprofessional. The homeowner becomes dissatisfied and refuses further payment on the contract. To his dismay, the owner then discovers that the contract, in fine print likely to be visible only under a laboratory microscope, contains interest rates of 25 percent or higher, along with other broker's fees and commissions, and has been sold to a bank which proceeds to foreclose on the property when full payment is not forthcoming.

The exploitation of home equity financing began to flourish during the 1980s. Congress, along with many states, removed the existing prohibition of unconscionable or "usurious" interest rates and finance charges on real estate and personal property loans. This "deregulation" movement, when coupled with discriminatory lending practices by banking institutions (known as "red lining"), served to create a magnet for unscrupulous finance companies who were drawn to those areas occupied by minorities, the poor, and the elderly. These groups were unable to secure conventional loans at prevailing interest rates principally because of their skin color or station in life. But their homes remained in need of repairs and they had sizable equity in their homes to secure loans. The loan sharks pursued them as relentlessly as the kind that swim in bloody waters.

Even though the law today prohibits the practice of red lining, there still exists an invidious Catch-22 situation created by the banks: Their discriminatory practices forced the poor and elderly to turn to home equity loan companies that negotiated outlandishly high finance charges and then sold the loans (known as the secondary market) to the very banks who refused to make the loans in the first instance. But those who were considered either socially inferior or poor credit risks were obligated to pay interest rates that would shock the conscience of the most blue-suited of barbarians. And under established legal rules, homeowners who had been swindled out of their savings to pay for poor quality or incomplete work had no recourse against the banks.

The banks, by purchasing the loans, were considered to be "holders in due course," and not responsible for any misconduct on the part of the home-repair contractors or the original finance company that initiated the loan. In 1994 Congress passed the Home Ownership and Equity Protection Act that provides some relief from lenders of high-cost mortgages. The new law imposed more detailed disclosures of contract terms. Under the act a borrower can move against the banks. The borrower is allowed to carry claims against the original loan-giver to banks that purchase the loan.

One case that achieved considerable publicity involved Caroline Berger, an African-American woman who resides in Roosevelt, New York. Mrs. Berger suffers from diabetes and is legally blind. She has had more than her share of hardship, having to care for, in her home, her mentally retarded granddaughter and her great-granddaughter who is afflicted with cerebral palsy. Mrs. Berger had owned her home for nearly twenty years and as of 1988 was living on roughly $1,800 a month. According to the law suit that was filed on her behalf, she was contacted by a home-improvement contractor who refused to leave her home until she signed a contract—one that she was unable to read because of her poor vision. The contract called for her to pay $15,800 for vinyl siding and trim, gutters, and three storm doors.

Mrs. Berger's affidavit stated that she was never advised that the work was secured by a mortgage on her home, nor was she ever given copies of the loan documents. According to Mrs. Berger, during the course of 1988 she was pressured into signing five home-improvement contracts that cost a total sum of $49,700. One of the contracts called for the construction of an outside deck that she was unable to climb due to her diabetic condition. Another contract was supposed to be for $5,800, but someone had changed the figure to $15,800. Ironically, one of the contracts called for the removal of some of the siding and one of the storm doors that the contractor had originally installed. The two companies who financed the contractor sold the contracts and mortgages to other banks and finance companies.

Mrs. Berger made payments of more than $12,000 for the work until she reached the point where she could no longer continue. A case worker who had been assigned to her by Catholic Charities became alarmed when she discovered that her client was ensnared in obligations that she could not afford. The case worker helped secure the services of an attorney who initiated a conspiracy law suit against eleven home-improvement contractors, finance companies, and banks that he charged with engaging in deceptive lending practices. Other homeowners who learned of the lawsuit have come forward with similar complaints against the same companies and a class action suit is now pending in the courts.

Eutha M. King, a 68-year-old woman who lives in Crown Heights, Brooklyn, shared a fate similar to that of Mrs. Berger. Surviving on her monthly Social Security checks, Ms. King was talked into obtaining a $25,000 home-repair loan by a door-to-door contractor who convinced her that she needed new electrical wiring and a remodeled kitchen. The contractor failed to disclose the fine print of the contract and duped her into believing that her monthly payments would be $900, not the $1,600 she was forced to pay to the bank that had purchased the contract.

The work performed by the contractor was shoddy and incomplete, forcing Ms. King to call upon friends and relatives to help make her kitchen serviceable. She also had to take in her grand-daughter and ask her relatives to help her make the monthly payments on the contract. The bank did not empathize with her predicament, and over the course of three years, periodically threatened to foreclose on the home she had owned for more than twenty-five years.

A report issued by the city of New York's Consumer Affairs Department indicates that Ms. King's nightmare experience was not unique. According to the report, during a seven-year period, more than 32,000 minority homeowners in the neighborhoods of Brooklyn, Queens, and the Bronx had been targeted and systematically deceived by home-improvement contractors who obtained mortgages with interest rates as high as 21 percent. In most cases, the work was unprofessional and incomplete, leaving the homeowners, most of whom were elderly and poor, to confront bankers who turned stone ears to their complaints.

It is understandable how those with physical impairments or limited language skills might be victimized by quick-talking hustlers. The notion, however, of healthy and, theoretically, wise individuals signing contract forms without reading the fine print or paying in full for work to be performed at a later time would appear as the height of irresponsibility. But few of us can claim immunity from acts of folly.

When I was a first-year law school student and about to become the proud father of a new baby boy, I was paid an unsolicited visit by a well-known maker of baby furniture. The salesman was professional in appearance and presentation. He showed me photographs of a beautiful (and expensive) crib, one that could, as our child grew older, be converted into a single bed. At the conclusion of his presentation, I was convinced that it probably could be expanded into a king-size bed by the time our son turned 18, and with a small motor installed perhaps even turned into a fin-tailed Cadillac that he could drive off to college. Additional bonuses included a play pen big enough for Tarzan to swing from and a three- or four-year supply of 8" x 10" color photographs to capture the beauty of his early years.

Now, I was quite a young man of the world (and a law student to boot) and I allowed that I was interested but wanted to discuss the proposal overnight with my wife. Ah, but then came the rub. The salesman was only permitted to make a one-shot presentation. The bonus features were included only if I signed that night, not twenty-four hours later. What a dilemma! We needed a crib for the baby. Surely the baby would quickly outgrow the crib and would be in need of a bed. And by the way, why not spend a little (actually, a lot) extra now and buy the best? Nothing is too good or expensive for our son!

Alas, even though my wife and I were surviving on an $8-a-week food budget, I signed the contract. At the time, we could afford the equivalent of a go-cart, but I decided to buy our son a Cadillac. I couldn't resist the pressure, the thought of losing the bonus items, of thinking how smart of me to acquire an all-in-one lifetime bed for our first-born. My vanities were exposed and fully exploited. Of course, almost immediately thereafter, I fell into the pit of buyer's remorse, but I rationalized away my regrets with a bravado that rang hollow inside my heart.

It was a lesson, however, well learned. Since that day, I have refused to permit unsolicited salesmen to darken my doorstep and have never fallen for the sales pitch that "this offer is good only until the end of business today." Tomorrow there always will be another sale.

⟶

Most states have established Consumer Fraud Divisions in the office of the attorney general. And many have passed tough consumer-protection laws that impose stiff civil and criminal penalties for those who engage in deceptive and fraudulent trade practices. But everyone, regardless of age, should take precautions to protect themselves from those who, like Danny DeVito's character, ask, "If you can't run scams, what's left?"

Dos and Don'ts

• Beware of home-improvement contractors who make unsolicited visits to your home.

• If you are in need of home improvements, obtain at least two or three estimates or bids for the work to be done.

• Do not do business with any contractor who is not bonded by state or local authorities.

• Check with your Better Business Bureau or the attorney general's office in your state to determine if any complaints have been filed against the contractor.

• Never sign any loan application with blanks, and before signing any contract be sure that you understand all of the terms, including the contractor's obligations of performance, quality of materials to be used, and the dates for completion of the work. Look specifically for hidden commissions and fees that may be buried in the fine print.

• Be wary of any lender who offers quick cash in return for holding title to your home as security for the loan. These proposals usually come from unlicensed finance and mortgage companies that charge high interest rates and will foreclose quickly if full payment of the loan is refused.

- Do not under any circumstances make full payment in advance of the work that is to be undertaken. Be sure to withhold a portion of the amount you are obligated to pay until you are satisfied that the work has been completed according to the terms of the contract. This should be more than a token amount in order to insure full compliance by the contractor.

- If possible, you should ask an attorney to review the contract, particularly if the amount of money involved is significant.

- Under most state laws, you have three business days to cancel the contract after signing it, even if the work has already been initiated (unless the work involves emergency repairs that you have authorized).

- If a bank or finance company is pressuring you for non-payment of a home-improvement loan, contact an attorney. You may be able to demonstrate that the work is incomplete or shoddy and therefore you are not liable for the balance that is claimed to be due.

CHAPTER FOUR

To Hear or Not to Hear?

———————————

The sound must seem an echo to the sense.

—*Alexander Pope*

Imagine a life without music or laughter, without the voices of children, the songs of birds, without even a simple conversation with a relative or friend. For an estimated 24 million Americans with impaired hearing, they need not call upon the powers of imagination; they know the reality of the encroaching "sounds of silence."

Hearing impairment or loss can affect the lives of young and old alike. It may be the product of a birth trauma,, genetic predisposition, viral or bacterial infection, a tumor, head trauma or occupational hazard. Problems associated with the outer or middle ear may be surgically corrected. For those with sensorineural or "nerve" hearing loss affecting the inner ear, surgery is rarely an option.

The diminution of the ability to hear is a natural part of the aging process. Those who served in the military and were exposed to percussive artillery blasts or the roar of jet engines are more likely candidates for hearing loss. So, too, are assembly-line workers who have gone without protection from the high-pitch racket of chattering machinery. We have yet to calculate the auditory damage done to "heavy metal" rock musicians and the millions of their fans who flock to concerts or spend hours replaying their CDs on high-volume stereophonic headsets. But even those who have spent a life in idyllic splendor and quietude are not immune from the taxes of time. About 30 to 50 percent of adults over the age of 65 suffer some degree of hearing loss, and that number increases to approximately half of those 75 or older.

A partial hearing loss can be helped with the use of a hearing aid—an electronic device that picks up sound waves with a small microphone and then amplifies the sounds, making them louder, sending them to the inner ear through a miniaturized speaker. Although hearing aids are among the top three items purchased by elderly consumers (along with eyeglasses and canes), only about 15 percent of those with hearing loss acquire them. Thus, as many as 18 million to 20 million people who could benefit from the use of hearing aids are going without them.

For many people, cost is the most critical factor. Most elderly consumers live on a fixed income that provides little flexibility in their budget. A hearing aid that can range from $600 for one to $3,500 a pair—*for which Medicare and most private insurers provide no coverage*—is well beyond the reach of many who could benefit from the device.

There is also the issue of vanity. While we think little of wearing eyeglasses—bi-focaled and tri-focaled—to correct vision deficiencies, the very thought of wearing a hearing aid is viewed by many as announcing to the world the triumph of advancing infirmity. Now, admittedly, some of the older model hearing aids are big and clunky. And the sight of those devices either hanging like anchors on the stems of eyeglasses or filling the entire ear canal is not likely to draw compliments as to their visual appeal. But the marvels of technology have reduced newer models to the size of a thumbnail and rendered them virtually invisible to prying eyes. We are likely to witness even greater breakthroughs in hearing-aid technology in the foreseeable future.

There are, however, other factors, in addition to vanity and cost, that may discourage greater use of hearing aids by people who are in need of assistance—namely, serious confusion over the restorative powers of the aids and fear of high-pressure sales techniques by dealers who are more interested in selling the hearing aids than in assessing the needs of the consumer.

While hearing aids do have the ability to enhance the quality of life for millions of Americans, parts of the hearing-aid industry have been plagued by misleading advertising, overly aggressive sales tactics, and shoddy testing by incompetent or abusive dealers. Far too many elderly have been sold hearing aids that they do not need, cannot afford, or cannot use. For first-time buyers, purchasing a hearing aid can prove more befuddling than walking through a carnival's house of mirrors.

The Food and Drug Administration (FDA) requires that hearing-aid dispensers advise consumers that it is in their best interest to visit a doctor before purchasing a hearing aid. In fact, the dispensers must obtain a written statement from a patient signed by a physician. The statement must verify that the patient's ears have been medically evaluated and the patient is approved for fitting with a hearing aid.

An adult patient can sign a waiver for a medical examination, but dispensers must avoid encouraging the patient to waive this requirement and advise the patient that such a waiver is not in the patient's best interest.

Rules of the Federal Trade Commission (FTC), in addition to prohibiting false and misleading advertising of products, also provide for a three-day cooling-off period. During this period, the sale can be canceled by the consumer and the seller must produce a full refund to the purchaser. This rule generally involves door-to-door sales but can be applied to other sales.

The FTC points out that the salesperson must tell you about your cancellation rights at the time of the sale and give you two copies of a cancellation form and a copy of your contract or receipt. You do not have to give a reason for wanting to cancel your purchase.

One particularly egregious abuse of these regulations involved a legally blind and hearing-impaired 92-year-old woman. A dealer visited her at home and coerced her into buying two hearing aids. The dispenser did not advise her against signing the waiver for a medical evaluation. And he literally put a pen in the woman's hand and guided her hand to the signature line even after she advised him that she could not read the sales contract. He proceeded to fill out her check and help her sign it.

Another example of an abusive sales technique involved Mr. Miles Kidd, a retired school teacher from West Virginia who visited a dealer after his daughter had seen a newspaper advertisement promoting the virtues of its product. Upon her urging, Mr. Kidd made an appointment for a free examination and evaluation. A receptionist wrote down a cursory history of his complaints, then directed him to a hearing specialist and assistant for an examination. Both the specialist and assistant stated that Mr. Kidd would eventually lose all ability to hear unless he purchased a hearing aid and insisted that it was necessary to purchase two aids in order adequately to detect the direction from which sounds were emanating.

Mr. Kidd did not fully succumb to the high-pressure tactics. He purchased only one hearing aid for the price of $975, exhausting most of his checking account. Immediately after the purchase, he began to experience problems. The hearing aid actually dulled rather than enhanced sounds. It dulled them to the point where he could hear better without the hearing aid than he could with it. He contacted the dealership to complain about the problem but was told that he simply was not used to wearing the hearing aid. Subsequent complaints fell on what can only be called "deaf ears."

Finally, exasperated with the treatment he had received, Mr. Kidd gave up and simply tossed the hearing aid into his desk drawer. Then, by chance, he read an article that revealed that the attorney general of his state was conducting an investigation into the dealership where he had purchased his hearing aid. He contacted the attorney general and filed a complaint.

After investigation, the Attorney General's Office determined that the dealership had:

- breached express and implied warranties with respect to the sale;
- violated his right to cancel the purchase agreement;
- failed to refer him to a physician or hearing specialist prior to fitting his aid;
- engaged in high-pressure, coercive tactics.

The end result was that Mr. Kidd obtained a refund of $850 from the manufacturer of the hearing aid.

Other consumers were bilked by the same dealership. One 84-year-old man went to have the batteries replaced in his hearing aid and was told that he really needed to buy a new set of aids that were far superior to the set that he owned. After a high-pressure sales presentation, he made a down payment, then went to his bank and borrowed $2,800 for the new aids. Shortly thereafter, when he experienced problems with one of the aids, he returned to the dealership and was given a replacement that was not custom-fitted; the dealer merely took it out of a drawer. The aids proved completely ineffective, so the man returned to his original pair. He had expended a total of $3,000 for hearing aids which now sit in a desk drawer in his home.

These are not isolated cases confined to one dealership. High-pressure hearing-aid selling is a nationwide problem complicated by the lack of adequate state certification standards, strict oversight and enforcement of a $1 billion industry, coupled with exaggerated claims and unrealistic expectations of consumers.

—

The FDA is considering revising the rule it promulgated in 1977 that requires a prior medical evaluation of a hearing-aid candidate, an evaluation that can be waived by an informed adult. This waiver was intended to be an exception to the general rule. In too many states, however, the exception has become the general rule. The FDA, for example, conducted a survey in the state of Vermont in 1991 of eleven hearing-aid dispensers and found that 55 percent of the purchasers waived the medical evaluation, and in 20 percent of the cases there were neither waivers nor physician statements in the patient files.

Dr. David Kessler, the current administrator of the FDA, who is both a pediatrician and an attorney, believes that consumers should be required to be examined by a licensed audiologist or another specialist with comparable qualifications before hearing aids can be sold to them, and that this requirement should be waived in very limited circumstances, if at all. He believes that general practitioners (MD)—or even specialists in a field other than that associated with otolaryngology (ears, nose, and throat specialty)—are not in the best position to make a comprehensive medical evaluation. It is his view that an audiologist possesses the professional education and skills to recognize whether underlying medical problems exist and can refer the consumer to an appropriate medical specialist for treatment.

Dr. Kessler is no stranger to controversy, and his opinions have stirred considerable opposition from those in the hearing-aid industry who note, among other things, that many rural states do not enjoy an abundance of certified or licensed audiologists. Therefore, if the non-audiologist hearing-aid dispensers who are currently licensed by state boards to conduct hearing loss evaluations are precluded from doing so, those in need of hearing aids will be discouraged from seeking them or deprived of securing relief.

Whether or not Dr. Kessler's views prevail or the FDA successfully alters its rules to prohibit waivers of the medical evaluation requirement, it is clear that some action to produce at least minimum standards of professional competency should be universal, if not uniform, among the states. For example, although audiologists are licensed in forty-two states, and hearing-aid dispensers licensed in forty-six states, Alaska, New York, and Washington, D.C. require only simple registration of hearing-aid dispensers. Massachusetts and Colorado do not impose any regulations on hearing-aid providers. Even among those states that require licensing, there are vast differences in the requirements demonstrating competency.

In a number of states, all that is necessary to obtain a license to sell hearing aids is proof that the applicant is 18 years old, has a high school diploma, is of good moral character, and has passed a simple examination.

One survey conducted by the American Association of Retired Persons (AARP) revealed that many dealers in Florida demonstrated more interest in sales than in securing the proper diagnosis for the consumer. AARP volunteers visited twenty-three hearing-aid sales operations in Tampa and West Palm Beach. After each visit the volunteers filled out forms that were analyzed by the Institute for Technology Development, a private research organization whose studies include the marketing of goods and services to older persons.

One participant, tested in a so-called "quiet room," complained that she could not hear the test tones because of the noise of passing traffic, car horns, a ringing telephone, and the hum of an air conditioner. The salesman shrugged. "You're not going to use your aid only in a quiet room are you?"

At another place, she reported, the salesman said he was a factory representative who happened to be there that day. "He told me I needed two hearing aids right away and had to place the order that day because he, the factory rep, wouldn't be back for three months. The cost of each aid was $2,000, but he could get me two for $3,500 and a 20 percent discount on top of that—if I bought that day."

The research showed that some dealers conducted tests in sound-proof booths while others conducted tests in open offices with the sounds of voices, telephone calls, or vehicular traffic permeating the room. Many evaluators failed to recommend that the consumers visit a physician for an examination before buying an aid. And few voluntarily offered thirty- or sixty-day trial periods and return policies in the absence of a demand by the consumers.

Although state and federal regulations specify certain examinations, testers reported that in 41 percent of their examinations a hearing aid was recommended without these examinations. The tests are designed to indicate whether the patient has a medically treatable condition.

One seller said that it was in the consumer's interest *not* to see a physician before buying a hearing aid. Another claimed that a hearing aid would "exercise the nerve and slow down the hearing loss." Don't worry about the thirty-day trial period, another said, since he was recommending a hearing aid with 24-karat gold circuits. Another refused to provide prices until the sale was made! And this in a state with some of the strongest hearing-aid regulations in the nation.

Add to these Florida practices the representations made by certain hearing aid manufacturers—their aids can filter out background noise or let you hear only what you wish to hear—and we can readily see how false expectations are so easily raised and so quickly dashed. Analog electronics and digital signal processing are improving the quality and capability of hearing aids dramatically, but there is no technology currently available that effectively eliminates background noise or restores hearing to complete normalcy. Advertisements claiming otherwise clearly constitute misleading and deceptive practices and have been withdrawn by the industry.

The International Hearing Society (IHS), which represents hearing-aid dispensers, maintains that the number of complaints filed about hearing aids with state authorities or private organizations such as the Better Business Bureau amounts to approximately 0.50 percent—among the lowest of any product category. It might be argued that this simply reveals that consumers believe that the fault lies with them rather than the equipment or that they are unaware that they have any legal recourse available to them. The IHS counters with the statement that the AARP surveys reflect a 79 percent satisfaction level among hearing-aid consumers.

It is unnecessary to resolve this dispute. As with other facets of the health care and equipment industry, the majority of providers act with professionalism and high ethical standards. But if the industry wishes to avoid a black eye because of the actions of a few miscreants, it will have to be in the forefront of those calling for reform. Many of the 3.4 million hearing-aid users are elderly and living on fixed incomes, and they predominate among those who feel that they have been mistreated. This constitutes more than a mere bagatelle.

Fortunately, organizations such as the American Speech-Language-Hearing Association (ASHA), Self Help for Hard of Hearing People, Inc. (SHH), and the American Academy of Otolaryngology are among those leading the effort to adopt meaningful reforms that will call for more stringent licensing requirements and enforcement mechanisms in order to insure that consumers are protected from the unscrupulous.

The best check against fraudulent or improper conduct in this $1 billion industry, however, is education and the exercise of common sense. There are many publications and public announcements that can help inform growing numbers of those in need of hearing aids what to look for—and look out for—in seeking relief for hearing loss.

Dos and Don'ts

- Be wary of door-to-door sales of hearing aids. Hearing evaluations conducted in one's living room or kitchen are clearly inadequate and invalid.

- Avoid mail-order purchasers. No company can provide a comprehensive evaluation or proper fitting over the phone or by mail.

- Consult a physician, preferably one who specializes in diseases of the ear (otolaryngolgogist or ear-nose-throat) to determine if there are underlying medical problems that can be treated medically or surgically.

- Consult an audiologist to determine the level of hearing loss you have suffered; get from him or her a recommendation of a hearing aid that will suit your needs. While most audiologists dispense hearing aids, their services may not be available in some rural areas. Therefore, be sure to deal with a reputable, licensed hearing aid dispenser in your community.

- Be skeptical of manufacturers that claim that, with their device, you'll hear only what you want to hear. The technology to achieve such a marvel has yet to be produced or perfected.

- Ignore announcements that arrive in the mail for your "free hearing test" appointment. Often these tests are "free" because the vendors are not licensed or qualified legally to perform or charge for diagnostic testing. In addition, you may be charged a higher price for the hearing aid that more than covers any sum for a proper examination and evaluation.

- Always insist upon written warranties for the product.

- Demand written assurances that the aids can be returned within thirty or sixty days if you are not satisfied with the product.

- If you fail to achieve satisfaction from the dealer, contact your Better Business Bureau, the Consumer Protection Division of your state's attorney general's office, the FTC, or the FDA.

- Request from AARP a copy of its *Guide to Hearing Aids*, along with its *Report on Hearing Aids, User Perspectives and Concerns* (1993). Or contact the American Speech-Language-Hearing Association for its brochure *How to Buy a Hearing Aid*.

CHAPTER FIVE

Gifts, Trips, and other Gems

A fool can no more see his own folly that he can his ears.
—William Makepeace Thackeray

It arrives in the mail. An envelope with a plastic window displaying your name in bold letters. The envelope has a certain heft to it, alerting you that a long message is contained inside, several pages at least.

Excitedly, you tear open the envelop and extract an announcement on expensive looking paper. Your heart skips a beat. The sender declares: Congratulations! You've just won $1 Million, a Mercedes Benz, a diamond the size of Plymouth Rock, or an all-expenses-paid trip to Papua, New Guinea . . . .

You are excited but confused. You don't recall entering a contest. Perhaps a son or daughter did so on your behalf. Perhaps your Social Security number was simply plucked out of a national lottery.

Perhaps. . . you'd better beware.

"Prize giveaways" and "sweepstakes" have become prime territory for scam artists who promise the moon, and send you, if you're lucky, a packet of green cheese. Their methods, while clever and diverse, share a common goal—to separate the naive and gullible from their money.

The "winner" of a valuable prize, for example, may be directed simply to call a toll-free number in order to claim the prize. When the call is placed, an automated voice instructs the caller to enter the "claim number" contained in the letter or postcard he or she received by hitting the corresponding keys on the telephone.

What arrives in the mail shortly thereafter is an extraordinarily large phone bill! The number originally called may have been "toll-free," but when the "claim number" was entered, it triggered access to an automated information center for which the caller was charged just as if he or she had called a 900 number for which there is either a flat fee charged or one that is based on a per minute rate of usage.

This scheme appears to be in direct violation of a new Federal Trade Commission (FTC) rule that requires print, radio, and television advertisements to contain, among other things, an up-front disclosure of the total cost of the call if there is a flat fee or a charge on a per-minute rate, along with any other fees that might be charged. The FTC rule also requires that those services that offer a consumer the chance to enter a sweepstakes by dialing a 900 number to win a prize must state the odds for winning or just how those odds are to be calculated. In addition, the advertisement must tell you that there is free way to enter the sweepstakes and provide you with instructions on how to enter free of charge or where to obtain that information.

A variation of this bait-and-switch to a 900 number scheme involves the consumer calling the toll-free number and talking to a smooth-talking telemarketer who persuades the caller to furnish his or her credit card number simply for "verification" purposes. Or the telemarketer may claim that the credit card must be used to pay for shipping or handling charges or taxes due to the government. It should come as no surprise—although it always does—that all the lucky winner receives is a cheap product, along with substantial credit card charges.

The FTC has uncovered and prosecuted a scheme in which elderly citizens were tricked into "paying hundreds of dollars for multi-year magazine subscriptions." The consumers were told that the magazines were free, except for postage or processing, that they were sent on trial, and that they could be canceled at any time.

The telemarketers, according to the FTC, "apparently convinced many elderly citizens that they were only entering sweepstakes or agreeing to receive something for free. When a sales agreement came in the mail, the consumer often thought it was junk mail, and did not realize the implication of failing to take steps necessary to cancel the subscription."

One scheme in Arkansas involved a company that targeted elderly consumers, promising them that they had won a "complete home entertainment center." The only condition imposed was a requirement that the winners purchase a six-month supply of vitamins. The "home entertainment center" consisted of a small radio-tape player worth about $20. The charge for the bottle of vitamins and grand prize was $800.

A Kentucky man expected to win a $1000 "hot tub" as a prize after having paid $800 for pen and pencil sets worth a few dollars. The hot tub turned out to be a small kiddy wading pool along with a device, described as resembling an "egg beater," that agitated the water.

One company operating nationwide principally has targeted elderly consumers to "guarantee" that they will receive one of five "major awards" such as $5,000 in cash, a "top-of-the-line home audio entertainment center," or a 10-karat diamond-and-sapphire bracelet if they purchase the company's merchandise. The company, using telemarketers who work from a well-honed script, advises the consumer that the firm needs proof that the consumer is an "active customer and not someone's friend or relative in the firm." So the customer is asked to send in a check for $649.50 and an order for an assortment of the company's "popular gift items."

"Right along with your order," says the telemarketer, "will be your major award, within about twenty-one working days."

What if the consumer initially resists the sales pitch? No problem. The telemarketers' script is designed to overcome anticipated skepticism. Here are some examples:

NO MONEY

Well, _____, if money is a bit tight for you, this couldn't come at a better time. I mean FIVE THOUSAND DOLLARS is not a lot of money, it's not going to change your life-style any, but it sure would help, wouldn't it? TRUST_____, I'll never lie to you or misrepresent anything to you for any monetary gain for myself or my company. I just don't believe in that. If I didn't know you would be happy with what you're getting, I wouldn't be on the phone with you right now. What you'll be receiving, you'll DEFINITELY be happy with, anybody would. So let the promotion fall into place for yourself, and when this is over, you'll be a customer or at least a friend, of _____, for life. I guarantee it, FAIR ENOUGH? (IF YES, GO TO CLOSE.)

GUARANTEE

Obviously, I'm not allowed to disclose which of the awards you're to receive. I wouldn't jeopardize my position for anyone. But I can tell you this, what you'll be receiving, you'll DEFINITELY be happy with, anybody would. You did very well in this promotion.

WHAT'S THE CATCH?
HOW MUCH IS THIS GOING TO COST ME?

Well, I will ask you for a small invoice [i.e, the check] but that's not the important thing. What is important, is that because you are guaranteed one of these major awards . . . we may have to use your picture in major magazine advertisements with the item you receive. But I can assure you that these advertisements will ONLY appear in respectable publications, like *Vogue, Cosmopolitan* or *People*. You don't have any objections to that do you?

SKEPTICISM

I can appreciate your skepticism _____, all that tells me is I'm speaking to an intelligent person. So let's speak intelligently. We're not asking you to reach into your back pocket and send us a bunch of money, and hope you get an award. There is no hope or luck involved in this promotion. That's the beauty of this promotion, is it has been pre-determined that you, _____, are guaranteed to receive one of the five top awards in the largest promotion in our company's history.

So do yourself a favor, let the promotion fall into place for yourself, and when it's all said and done you'll be calling me back to say thanks. FAIR ENOUGH?

JUST A CONTEST

_____, if this were just a contest or drawing, I wouldn't be on the phone wasting your time. You are absolutely guaranteed one of the five major awards, as I already stated, and let's say, for instance, you get the fifth award, the $2,500 cashier's check, granted, it's not going to put you on easy street, but it is certainly worth a small order and a picture, so take the package and get your award so I can get your photograph. FAIR ENOUGH?

WHY DO I HAVE TO BUY?

_____, the company asks you to place an order for two reasons, one, we couldn't use your picture saying that you are a customer of ours if you really aren't, and two, the most important reason, is because you're not taking any chances.You are guaranteed a major award. You can't lose. FAIR ENOUGH?

HARD-EARNED MONEY

_____, I wouldn't ask you to part with your hard-earned money without the knowledge that your money is being well spent. That's why my company puts your award right in the box along with our top of the line executive gift products, and the beauty of it all is that not one more penny leaves your pocket. There are no hidden charges in our promotion. We pay all shipping, handling, freight and insurance. It all comes out to you by the U.P.S. Pre-paid. FAIR ENOUGH?

WE STAND BEHIND EVERYTHING

We stand behind everything we say and everything we send out—100 percent. If there's any problem at all, call our toll-free number and we'll do whatever it takes to make it right. FAIR ENOUGH?

NO MONEY-BACK GUARANTEE

How would it look when one of our customers receives a $5,000 cashier's check and told everyone that we gave him/her a great award but he/she sent the product back? We can't give you a money-back guarantee because you're guaranteed a major award, but let's say this, if you're not happy for any reason, give us a call and we'll do whatever it takes to make you happy. FAIR ENOUGH?

OVER THE PHONE

You watch TV and I'm sure you see the commercials where you can call an 800 number and order merchandise over the phone and send in a check or money order. The reason you can safely deal with those companies, as well as this one, is your check is a legal receipt and fully protects you as a customer to receive your product and your award. FAIR ENOUGH?

HOW CAN YOU AFFORD
TO GIVE OUT MAJOR AWARDS?

_____, the best way I can make sense of this is to explain it this way. Let's say you get the $5,000 cashier's check, a picture of you and your award in my catalog will bring me a hundred new customers who spend an average of a thousand dollars each, that's $100,000. Then it's well worth my effort to give you one of these five awards. I only ask two things, enjoy the award and give me your word that I'll get a good clear picture for my catalog. FAIR ENOUGH?

Fair enough? Not really. The gift items that arrive are dramatically inferior to the "fabulous" ones described by the telemarketers. Usually, they are cheap pen and pencil sets and calculators worth a few dollars. And the "major awards" similarly turn out to be major disappointments. The genuine 10-karat diamond-and-sapphire bracelet described as being worth more than $1,000 may have an appraised value of under $100. And the "home entertainment center," that prompts visions of five-foot-high speakers, a 500-watt Bose AM-FM stereo radio and cassette deck, along with a 10-slot compact disc player, is little more than a reconditioned turntable and cassette player worth less than $100.

Polls indicate that 92 percent of Americans have been contacted in prize postcard schemes. One survey found that 29 percent (53 million people) have responded to the solicitations. Of those who responded, 69 percent (37 million people) received no prize, and those who received a prize were deeply disappointed over the disparity between what was promised and what was received.

Now the accumulation of years is supposed to be accompanied by wisdom. But if "experience is the name we give to our mistakes," then it's legitimate to ask, how can those who should know better be taken in by such scams?

Mr. Archie Wilcox of Duluth, Minnesota, who had served as president of Minnesota Seniors for three years, offered some insight into this question. He suggested that an element of hypnotism is involved. "They capture your mind," he said. "They're doing you great favors when they take your money, but there's an urgency to act right now . . . .The delay may cost you winning a prize."

Like so many other victims, Mr. Wilcox was led to believe that the golden ring of opportunity was coming his way and he had just one last opportunity to grab it. He had worked hard all his life. He had scrimped and saved. Now he had the chance, not only to preserve his savings, but to multiply them. Expensive, official-looking stationery had arrived by mail, advising him that he had won something wonderful—a large sum of money, a trip around the world, a diamond bracelet. Excited over the prospect that life's roulette wheel had picked his lucky number, he responded to the literature.

Almost immediately thereafter, he began to receive phone calls congratulating him on his good fortune. Just how much money, the caller would ask, did he have in his savings account? After obtaining his monetary status, the caller would breathlessly urge him to send in his check in order to claim his prize. In other words, he had to purchase his prize!

Did Mr. Wilcox fall for this scheme? Yes, "hook, line, and sinker." He sent the telemarketer a check for $4,000. The attorney general's office in Minnesota has managed to secure the return of $300 of his money, and while Mr. Wilcox was grateful for the assistance he has received from the state, his recovery to date amounts to little more than a "drop in the bucket."

Mr. Wilcox might have done well to heed the warning from his wife, who recognized from the outset that these prize giveaways were mere scams. Predators always seem to know where to strike to hit the most vulnerable spot in their victims. Usually, it can be found in the ego. Mr. Wilcox considered himself an "unimportant person," an average citizen, perhaps even below average. Now this opportunity would lift him above his station in life—if only he acted quickly. And, too, there was an element of desperation in his decision. His car had 185,000 miles on it. He wanted to trade it in, but would need cash beyond his monthly Social Security check to use for car payments.

Mr. Wilcox suggests that women have a certain innate advantage in detecting the difference between the legitimate and the fraudulent. "We, as men, are the supermen, but we aren't quite as super as we think we are. That's why we have wives."

There's a good deal of truth in Mr. Wilcox's humble concession. But women are not immune to the solicitations of the unscrupulous. The attorney general of Minnesota related the story of "Mary," a 79-year-old woman who had a limited ability to read and was considered to be legally blind.

Mary was contacted by "Opportunities Unlimited," a company that invited her to enter a contest to win large cash prizes. She simply had to send in $10 or $20 for the chance to answer simple, unchallenging questions. Not long after Mary responded to the first solicitation, she was advised that she had cleared the first hurdle and was well on her way to victory. More solicitations came, not only from Opportunities Unlimited, but from a horde of other pirate operations. Mary's name had entered the sinkhole world where all the parasites dwell. She had been placed on the "suckers lists."

By the time the attorney general learned of her case, Mary had lost $5,000 to Opportunities Unlimited and a grand total of $25,000. She had lost all of her savings, was forced to live off her Social Security checks, and had even gone without food in order to keep paying the entry fees for the prize contests. The solicitations simply kept coming, often involving as many as thirty-two phone calls a day, forcing her, finally, to obtain an unlisted number. This is not an unusual case.

An 80-year-old Maine woman was solicited a second time after having fallen for a telemarketing scheme (this is known as "reloading"). It is a common strategy employed by telemarketers to exploit the disappointment of the consumer who may be inclined to try to "win back" what he or she failed to acquire through the first solicitation. The woman declared that she was not interested. For a period spanning three days, the company continued to call her every few minutes beginning at 8 a.m., with the calls continuing until she was forced to turn on her answering machine. This practice, which constitutes harassment and violates the laws of many states, is designed to beat down and beleaguer the consumer to the point that he or she agrees to send in the requested amount of money simply to stop the phone calls.

"Often the names of victims of one scam are sold to other promoters and used to develop a second target list," states Kenneth M. Hearst, assistant chief postal inspector for criminal investigations. "We recently arrested the promoters of a Denver "boiler room" who used the names of elderly participants in an alleged contest to swindle them in a second contest where large prizes were offered only to those who bought home security systems at a cost of nearly $600."

"And, if any one case could illustrate the rapacious nature of the boiler-room bandits, it is a current criminal case we are completing. . . . The "pitch" is directed to persons who are swindled by other boiler rooms. The recycled victims are told the legitimate telemarketing industry wants them to make up for the sins of its few bad members by sending them cash or a valuable gift. Of course, they must pay an alleged "gift tax" in advance. To date, over $250,000 in phony gift taxes have been collected by the promoters."

The devil is always said to be lurking in the details of any deal. This is particularly so in the dream-come-true travel scams that are marketed over the telephone. One lucky person in Wisconsin won a vacation in Hawaii. Unfortunately, the vacation included the price of the hotel but not the transportation. The caveat buried in the fine print of the "prize" required the purchase of regular airfare to Hawaii, the cost of which was approximately $2,000 for two people.

A scheme frequently utilized by fraudulent travel con-artists is to instruct you to call a toll-free number for details about the "free trip" you have just won. Once the call is placed, you're advised that you must join a travel club in order to qualify for the trip. Of course, there'll be a request for your credit card number so you can be billed directly for the club membership fee. Once in "the club," you'll receive a vacation packet of information containing instructions for making reservations for your "pre-paid trip."

Should you ever arrive at your dream spot, you may find to your dismay that you have no place to stay since your reservations were never confirmed directly with the hotel. Or it may be that before you can board a jet from O'Hare, LAX, or LaGuardia airports heading to London, Hawaii, or New Zealand, you discover that you can't afford to meet the heavily camouflaged restrictions or high-priced conditions attached to the prize offer.

A common trick requires the consumer to join a travel club— with membership fees ranging from $50 to $400—before receiving a round-trip air travel ticket for one and lodging for two, let's say, in Hong Kong or Kuala Lumpur in Malaysia. The catch here is detectable, but not necessarily obvious. For the second person to accompany you, you'll be required to purchase an expensive round-trip ticket that will far exceed the price you could acquire from a reputable travel agency or from the bargains offered directly by the airlines.

Even though strong consumer protections have been enacted, there will still be those telemarketers who try to scam their customers. As one attorney general responsible for prosecuting these cases noted, telemarketing crooks are "a lot like cockroaches: When you chase them out of one location, they run somewhere else."

A few sensible rules will keep you from being a victim of telemarketing fraud.

Be wary of unsolicited mail or telephone calls that announce: CONGRATULATIONS! YOU HAVE JUST BEEN SELECTED TO WIN A GRAND PRIZE. . . . There are no free lunches and there are no companies in the business of giving you something for nothing. The shipping and handling fees and taxes may well exceed your prize or gift.

Callers offering prizes are required to disclose the odds of winning and that no purchase is necessary to win, as well as the nature of the prize. If you don't hear these disclosures, hang up.

Be sure to ask for information about the organization or company and request that it send you written material about the business. Never judge a book by its cover and never assume that the organization is legitimate simply because it wraps its offer in an expensive-looking brochure or prints a letter on quality stationery.

Ask questions. Get as much information as you can. Learn about the total cost of the item or service you are getting and any special terms or conditions that apply in order to get the prize or item that is the subject of the call. Also ask questions and get information about how you can get a refund, exchange goods, or get credit for a returned purchase. Ask if the sale is final and your money nonrefundable. If a prize is offered, ask about the odds of winning, the value of the prize, and whether any payment is necessary to "win."

If the call involves an investment opportunity, ask about the risk, liquidity, earnings potential, or profitability of the investment being offered. Be very careful about authorizing a telemarketer to debit your bank account to pay for the item or service. Do not authorize such a debit by the telemarketer unless you are confident about the reputation of the seller and have faith in the value of the item you are purchasing. While you may eventually get your money back if the telemarketer has scammed you or you are dissatisfied with your purchase, it could take a long time to get your problem settled. It is best not to take a chance if you have any suspicions about the caller.

If the caller refuses to answer any of your questions, hang up. If the calls continue, report the organization to the attorney general of your state. Check with your local Better Business Bureau or the consumer protection office of your state attorney general to determine if any complaints are on file against the organization. Even if no complaints have been filed, however, you should not accept this fact as evidence of legitimacy since many fraudulent operators change names and their place of doing business.

Never, under any circumstances, give out your credit card number or any information associated with it—such as the expiration date—

over the telephone unless you are satisfied that you are doing business with a reputable company.

There is no reason for you to make an immediate decision. If the caller is legitimate, you'll be offered enough time to make an informed decision. Never send cash, a check, or money order by courier or overnight delivery service to a telemarketer insisting on immediate payment. Not only will your money be likely to disappear, but it will make it harder for law enforcement authorities to assist you in their recovery efforts.

If you've been the victim of telemarketing fraud, swallow your pride and report it. You are only one of the many millions who fall prey to the unscrupulous. And, if you are a victim, alert your friends and neighbors to your experience. Silence may conceal your embarrassment, but it will also allow them to suffer a similar fate.

—

The dimensions of telemarketing fraud cannot be accurately quantified. One study concluded that only one in 10,000 victims report telemarketers to law enforcement officials. Most are simply too ashamed to admit to anyone that they have been duped. But there is little doubt that the problem is growing dramatically. According to the FBI, telemarketing fraud is costing consumers as much as $40 billion a year. While federal and state laws pertaining to this type of fraudulent activity are being adopted and vigorously enforced, many of these telemarketing scams are going international in an effort to evade our laws.

Canadian conmen working out of Toronto, for example, recently persuaded an elderly Maine man to invest in indium, a metal that was hawked as a "strategic" metal, but was, in reality, little more than an inexpensive metal used for dental fillings. He was persuaded to make this investment in response to slick brochures and even a videotape of a CNN report on the metal. He wrote a check for $1,368 for twenty ounces of the metal. This turned out to be ten times its actual value of $110. He was fortunate to obtain a return of his money through a cleverly disguised reverse scam conceived and carried out by Maine's securities administrator. Most victims have not been so lucky.

Congress recently passed legislation to protect consumers against deceptive and abusive telemarketing practices, and the Federal Trade Commission has issued rules to enforce these new protections. See "Dos and Don'ts" at the end of this chapter to learn about some of the rights that went into effect December 31, 1995, under the new FTC rules.

The passage by Congress of telemarketing fraud legislation will go far in dealing with hucksters who move from state to state in order to avoid prosecution, but legal actions against "boiler room" operations whose tentacles originate from beyond our borders will prove more difficult to tackle, since enforcement based on international law raises difficult issues to resolve. Unless we have cooperative agreements or bilateral treaties with the other countries from where the telemarketers are operating, then there may be no way to bring the perpetrators to justice or seek restitution on behalf of the defrauded.

There is no law that prohibits an individual or company from soliciting business by telephone. Indeed, given the world of instant communications in which we live, it may be preferable for many to conduct business in this fashion. But as in any other situation, *the buyer must always beware*—particularly when dealing with strangers or anonymous callers. Remember, if it's easy money that you're offered, it's yours that they have in mind.

Dos and Don'ts

Restrictions on Telemarketers

- Telemarketers are not allowed to place calls before 8 a.m. and after 9 p.m. or call customers who have said they don't want to be called.

- Telemarketers are required promptly to disclose at the beginning of the call that they are making a sales call, identify the seller, the nature of the goods or services they are offering, and, if it is a prize promotion, the fact that no purchase is necessary to win.

- Before telemarketers can ask consumers for credit card or bank account information or arrange for a courier to pick up payment, they must disclose to the customer the total costs of the item or service being bought, the terms of getting a refund or exchange, and, in the case of a prize promotion, the odds of winning.

- Telemarketers are not allowed to debit consumers' checking accounts without express consent. The telemarketers can obtain consent by either written authorization from the customer or by taping the conversation with the customer and making the tape available to the customer's bank upon request.

- Telemarketers are specifically prohibited from misrepresenting key aspects of prize promotions, such as the odds of winning, the nature and value of the prize, or whether a payment is required to win. They are also strictly prohibited from misrepresenting investment opportunities, including the risk, earnings, and liquidity of investments being offered.

CHAPTER SIX

Risky Business

Fortune, that with malicious joy
Does man her slave oppress,
Proud of her office to destroy
It seldom pleas'd to bless.

— *John Dryden*

Yogi Berra, the Yankee baseball legend, who could catch an insight as well as a high inside fast ball, once said, "You can hear a lot, just by listening." The corollary, of course, is that you can see a lot, just by watching. When it comes to investing in the stock market, you should pretend that you're approaching a railroad crossing: *Stop, Look, and Listen.* Too many people have failed to heed the warning and, as a result, have met with financial disaster.

Most senior citizens are necessarily cautious and protective of their savings. Being retired and without the ability actively to produce greater income, they must rely on that generated by savings or investments to supplement their pensions or Social Security checks. But they have been caught in a good news/bad news dilemma. Interest rates, which once raged at 21 percent levels in the late 1970s and early 1980s toppled into a free fall. While this was, and remains, good news for the overall economy and especially for members of the younger generations that find it easier to purchase homes and other products for their families, low interest rates have made it difficult for seniors who live on fixed incomes to keep up with inflation or pay for contingencies such as a major operation, expensive prescription drugs, or catastrophic illness.

Savings accounts, Certificates of Deposit (CDs), and Money Market Funds, once the great repository of seniors' savings, have become less attractive due to their low returns or long periods of maturity. The interest rate on passbook accounts and CDs have taken a plunge in recent years, requiring senior citizens to shop around for other types of investments. Consequently, the securities market has become a popular choice for the small—and very often unsophisticated—investor.

The securities industry, responding to increased demand, has generated a vast array of financial instruments which have all the clarity of Stephen Hawking's explanation of the creation of the cosmos. As a result, investors have had to turn to an army of brokers, sales representatives, financial consultants, and advisers to guide them to safety through this dark, murky universe. Unfortunately, among these professionals boasting sterling silver badges are pirates and predators, ready to rob all voyagers of their possessions.

Charles Keating is a name that will live in infamy. He was the chairman of the board of Lincoln Savings American Continental Corp., which among other misdeeds, sold over $250 million of unsecured bonds to some 23,000 investors, many of whom were elderly and of limited financial means. He has been convicted of fraudulent activity and sentenced to prison, but no punishment can be considered harsh enough to compensate for the pain and suffering Mr. Keating inflicted on the vulnerable and unsuspecting.

Mr. Keating was not the only high flyer in the investment world who lined his pockets with the savings of the needy. In 1993, the SEC imposed stiff sanctions against Paine Webber, charging the firm with direct theft of customer funds, trading in the accounts of customers known to be dead, making trades that the customers never wanted, excessively trading accounts to generate commissions, lying to customers about the value of their accounts, fraudulently filling out customer account documents, and selling unregistered securities. It was not just a case of unsupervised stockbrokers engaging in a bit of "white collar wilding." Kidder Peabody's top government bond trader allegedly conducted up to $350 million in bogus trades before being apprehended in 1994. And prior to the disclosure of Paine Webber's skullduggery, there were the transgressions of some of the nation's most prestigious investment banking firms such as Salomon Brothers, Drexel Burnham Lambert Inc., and E.F. Hutton.

Indeed, Prudential-Bache Securities pushed more than $8 billion worth of risky limited partnerships into the marketplace during the 1980s and peddled them as safe and profitable investments. The sales produced profits in excess of $1 billion for the firm.

It is important to note that these cases do not involve "boiler room" or hit-and-run operators who either sweet-talk or browbeat their way into a senior citizen's living room and bank account, but licensed and ostensibly professionally trained brokers.

Investors must understand and remember that when they step into the brave new world of the financial marketplace they will not have the protection of the Federal Deposit Insurance Corporation (FDIC). You and your money are at the mercy of Darwinian forces where survival goes to the smartest, the fastest, and the most fit. Put more bluntly, if you're looking for a big payoff, then you must be prepared to make a big pay out. You can lose it all!

In 1994, the mutual fund industry's assets reached trillion- dollar proportions with about 3,500 funds, qualifying it as the nation's third largest financial industry. At least one quarter of American families (26 million households) own shares in one or more of the funds on the market. Many are unsophisticated investors who do not understand that *mutual funds are not risk free and are not federally insured.*

A mutual fund pools the money of investors in order to purchase securities, such as stocks and bonds. When investing in a mutual fund, you are actually buying shares of an "investment company" whose sole function is to make the investments. The mutual funds, by diversifying investments, are designed to take much of the confusion and some of the risk out for individuals who want to invest in the stock market. The types of investments made by the fund will reflect the level of risk to the investors. The fund's investments will be governed by its objectives which are required by law to be stated in a prospectus.

While mutual funds, properly managed, do offer a degree of safety to investors, there are at least four dangers that need to be considered

1. Interest-rate risk: When interest rates rise, the value of bonds and other interest-bearing investments falls. Therefore, if a mutual fund invested in certain bonds, and the interest rate rises, the fund itself could decline.

2. Credit risk: The bonds of some companies pay double-digit interest rates, but to obtain these returns, investors must be willing to accept some chance for default.

3. Prepayment risk: When interest rates fall, individuals are not the only ones who consider the refinancing of existing debt. All borrowers prefer to issue new, lower-cost debt to pay off older, higher-priced debt. Companies may even "call" their bonds, leaving investors to settle for a lower yield after they are forced to reinvest.

4. Currency risk: An investor who leaps for, let's say, a 15 percent return on Mexican treasury bill mutual funds, can fall from a high yield into a 5 percent loss should the Mexican government devalue the peso by 20 percent—not exactly something as improbable as a Stephen King nightmare.

Fees

The prospectus for a mutual fund must have a fee table that explains the fund's costs. Fee tables are one way to compare the costs of different funds.

A fee table breaks the cost into two categories: (1) sales loads and transaction fees, and (2) ongoing expenses. The first category includes fees charged when you buy, sell, or exchange shares. In the second category are costs paid while you are in the fund.

Let's look at **sales loads.** "No-load funds" do not charge sales loads. In such a fund, you make your own choices. (Even in a no-load fund, however, there are ongoing expenses, such as management fees.)

The Securities and Exchange Commission (SEC), a highly reliable source of mutual fund information, offers the following definitions and explanations of sales loads:

When a mutual fund charges a sales load, it usually pays for commissions to the people selling the fund's shares and for other marketing costs. Sales loads buy a broker's services, including advice. But this does not guarantee superior performance. Funds that charge sales, according to the SEC, have not performed better than those that do not charge sales loads.

A **front-end load** is a sales charge paid when you buy shares. The law puts a cap of 8.5 percent on this type of load, which reduces the amount of your investment in the fund. (Put $1,000 in a fund with a front-end charge of 5 percent and $950 will actually go into the fund, with $50 going to pay the sales charge.)

A **back-end load** (also called a **deferred load**) is a sales charge paid when shares are sold. It usually starts out at 5 percent or 6 percent for the first year and gets smaller each year after that until it reaches zero in, say, the sixth or seventh year of your investment.

More than 300 administrative, civil, and criminal actions have been initiated by state agencies in the past several years against investment companies, broker-dealers, and sales agents of mutual funds, reflecting an unprecedented level of local concern on behalf of investors.

An examination of the allegations of impropriety lodged against one mutual fund company provides some understanding as to why this heightened level of anxiety may be justified. This company offers numerous mutual funds and also manages and sells insurance products. During the late 1980s and early 1990s, the company had approximately $3.5 to $4 billion in assets under management for roughly 270,000 clients.

Investors, many of them elderly and of limited investment experience, have alleged that the company used misleading and deceptive sales tactics, falsely represented bond funds as safe, prudent investments, and failed to disclose the high risks inherent in such funds—all of which caused the investors to suffer major losses when the national "junk bond" market went into decline in the late 1980s.

Mrs. Minnie Lou Pharr, a retired court reporter from Walls, Mississippi, and her husband, a retired postal worker, are but two of the fund's many victims, who can be found from Maine to California. In the mid 1980s, the Pharrs, whose only previous experience with investments was confined to bank certificates of deposit, became interested in enhancing their income once they both were retired. Upon the advice of a friend, they agreed to meet with a salesman of an investment company at their home.

The Pharrs explained that because of their approaching retirement, they did not want to invest in anything that put their principal at risk. The salesman recommended that they purchase a bond investment through his company. He assured them that these bonds paid a fixed rate of 12 percent interest, compared to the 7 percent or 8 percent return on bank CDs and that this rate would continue at least to the year 2000. The Pharrs were advised that although the investment was not covered by FDIC insurance, the bond's fixed rate of return made it "just as good" as if it was insured by the federal government. There was just no way they could lose.

They placed their trust and their money in the salesman, agreeing to invest $10,000 from Mr. Pharr's retirement program in addition to making monthly payments for a period of ten years. Although the salesman did furnish a prospectus and slick brochures declaring that the investment was appropriate for the full range of financial goals, he did not disclose or discuss the fees or commissions that the Pharrs would be obligated to pay. It was not long before they received a punch to their financial solar plexus. To their dismay, they discovered that they had not purchased bonds but shares in a company that invested in stocks and bonds. As the value of those shares fluctuated, the Pharrs' investment continued to decline.

The 12 percent rate of return the Pharrs had been promised had fallen to 8 percent, leaving them with $9,000 less in projected income from their $24,000 investment. They were successful in pulling $16,000 out from the "bond investment," but were forced to leave $10,000 in the fund because of law suits pending against the company. Instead of enjoying their retirement years, the Pharrs were left to face the prospect of selling the home they had lived in for twenty-three years. Their future would be one filled with anguish and anxiety.

This is a sad story, but one that is writ large and wide. The state of Maine, home of the shrewd Yankee traders, has suffered its share of exploitation.

In 1991, an 86-year-old man and his 79-year-old wife invested $29,000 into so-called high-yield funds, unaware that the funds were investing in junk bonds. Approximately a year later, they had lost $10,000 on their investment.

A couple, who had at one time been farmers but were forced to work at paper mill following a bad crop, invested $26,000 from a lump sum distribution and an IRA into a fund. They told the salesperson that this was the only money they would ever have and must be careful not to lose it. They were assured that the investment was safe and guaranteed to be better or just as good as a bank. The promise was gilded but not gold. They lost $9,000 of their life savings.

Another couple in their 60s—the husband was a heavy equipment operator for a paper company and his wife a grocery store clerk—invested $28,500 in a fund and were told during the sales presentation that the investment compared to a bank account, only it had more benefits. They lost several thousand dollars.

The cases are too numerous to detail. All told, approximately 5,000 investors' accounts were opened in the state of Maine alone, with overall losses conservatively estimated to be in excess of $1 million. It is clear from these cases that the individuals who have been victimized are neither wealthy nor well educated in the complex world of Wall Street. They were seniors who had accumulated a small nest egg to carry them to the end of their lives. They were looking for a warm safe haven and, in many cases, ended up out in the bitter cold as a direct result of placing trust in those who were either outright bandits who indulged in clever half-truths or incompetent salespersons whose only expertise consisted of reading a prepared script.

Maine was not the only state to seek legal redress against the company that put these people out in the cold. Eight states instituted administrative, civil, or criminal actions against this company, alleging among other things, misrepresentation in the sale of the funds sold by the company. Fifteen states entered into settlement agreements with the company for losses incurred by its investors. The allegations range from deception in sales pitches to incompetency and inadequacy in the training of salespersons selling the funds who frequently operated from a prepared script but had no real experience or expertise in the financial world.

The Securities and Exchange Commission entered into a settlement with the company, requiring it to pay nearly $25 million into a nationwide restitution fund to be used to satisfy claims of investors. One expert estimated that the investors' losses totaled $400 million.

A further complication has been added to the challenges facing those who are seeking higher returns on their capital—the entry of banks into the sale of securities.

Following the stock market crash in 1929, Congress passed legislation that erected a wall between banks and brokerage houses, preventing banks from selling securities because of the belief that stock speculation had provoked widespread bank failures. Over the years, that wall—much like the Berlin Wall—has come tumbling down. It is not surprising that banks are desperately trying to keep their customers from pulling money out of their institutions by offering alternatives to CDs or other insured savings accounts.

With relatively small returns on CDs and savings accounts, banks need new products and services to retain and attract customers. Bank executives argue that they must offer these uninsured products to keep their customers from investing elsewhere, such as at a brokerage firm or directly with a mutual fund company. Some banks have recently purchased or merged with large brokerage companies.

In 1993, banks sold about $92 billion worth of mutual funds to bank customers. Some banks gave their brokers financial incentives, such as high commissions for selling certain bank funds. These incentives often have the effect of inducing the broker to ignore the suitability of uninsured products to some customers, particularly those who are elderly. Some funds, for example, require a long-term commitment and may be wholly inappropriate for an older customer.

Former and current bank brokers at four major multistate banks admitted to targeting older customers who had savings accounts and certificates of deposit with the banks. The brokers viewed these customers as a prime market for the sale of uninsured products—even though they knew that these products may be inappropriate investments for these unsuspecting customers.

While we should not foreclose banks from selling securities, there are special dangers and problems associated with this new trend— namely, a tremendous potential for confusion by bank customers about the nature and safety of the investments they are purchasing. Surveys have shown that the vast majority of bank customers are unaware that mutual funds, stocks, and annuities sold at their banks are not insured by the FDIC. Most customers seem to believe that because they are dealing with a bank they are not taking any financial risk at all.

The banking industry has established a voluntary compliance program for full disclosure to bank customers and guidelines on the proper marketing of uninsured products. Unfortunately, there is substantial evidence that some banks are ignoring the guidelines and playing on their customers' confusion and deliberately steering them toward risky investments. Some of the practices include:

- Bank tellers **"cold calling"** customers whose CDs are about to mature and peddling annuities under false pretenses.
- Bank employees, in violation of customer confidentiality, **providing brokers the names and bank account information of customers** who have made large bank deposits. For this service the brokers pay referral fees.
- Banks giving **high commissions**, vacation trips, or other incentives to brokers who sell the bank's own mutual funds, regardless of whether they are suitable investments for the customer.
- Banks giving confusing and **misleading information** to cus-

tomers **about the safety of investments** being sold on bank premises.

- Some banks **aggressively targeting elderly customers** to purchase uninsured investments without fully disclosing the risks involved.

Ms. Leilani Jaskinski DeMint of St. Petersburg, Florida, a toll booth operator who lives with her 28-year-old autistic son, was an alleged victim of exploitation. Ms. DeMint and her mother had scrimped and saved for years in order to provide for her son's future. After her mother was killed in an auto accident, Ms. DeMint placed her entire savings in CDs in several banks and a credit union. She did not want to take any risks with her money.

When one of her CDs matured at her bank, she called a number of banks in the area to determine which was paying the highest interest rates. A man from her bank called and advised her that he could get her a higher rate than any other bank and persuaded her to come to the bank and meet with him.

When she arrived, he presented her with a card that contained the bank's name. At no time, she stated, did he ever indicate that he was a broker. He said that she could obtain a higher interest rate by having the bank purchase government bonds for her. He assured her that although the interest rate might fluctuate, her principal would not be in danger. Based upon his representations that her money was safe, Ms. DeMint signed papers transferring the $57,000 from her CDs and wrote a check for another $3,000 as the man suggested that deposits should be made in even increments.

She was advised that she would have to keep her money invested for a period of five years or suffer a penalty for early withdrawal. This was quite agreeable to her since her CDs also had penalties imposed for early withdrawals. She received a receipt for $60,000. Approximately a month later, she deposited another $10,000 from her credit union into the same bank, and again, received only a deposit slip.

Several months later she became suspicious when she received a statement from a company she had never heard of previously. The company advised her that she had earned $2,000 in interest and had a balance of $61,000 in her account. Ms. DeMint was understandably confused. When the company explained that she had purchased mutual funds and that she was lucky that she had not lost more of her principal, she turned to the bank that she had relied upon for advice. Rather than offering a comforting hand, the bank, instead, gave her a hard slap. She could withdraw the money from the account but she would have to pay the penalty. It was her problem, not theirs.

Not only did Ms. DeMint lose 10 percent of the money that she and her mother had worked so hard to save, but she had to pay taxes on the money that the bank claimed was interest on the investment.

Ms. DeMint may have been naive in placing her trust in her bank, but she was very clear on exactly what she wanted—to protect her principal at all costs. Moreover, she was not alone in having been misled by the bank. Others had similar experiences and similar losses.

Undoubtedly, all consumers, including senior citizens, have an obligation to ask serious questions and make informed decisions when they are offered deals that are too good to be true or are given a hard sales pitch. But just as consumers must take responsibility for their investment decisions, banks and brokers must not be allowed to play "hide the ball" with their customers when marketing uninsured investments. Concealing disclosure signs behind potted plants in their bank lobbies, writing disclosures that the investments are not covered by FDIC in microscopic print, or engaging in other practices designed to confuse or potentially mislead their customers cannot be allowed to go unchecked or unpunished.

Dos and Don'ts

• Do your homework on every investment. Be sure that you understand the risks associated with the investment.

- Define your own investment goals. Do not depend upon a broker, banker, or financial consultant to dictate your objectives.

- Never give a broker complete control over your money. If the broker or investment adviser says "just leave it all to me," the chances are very good that you will do precisely that. Be sure to follow your investment carefully, and never hesitate to question your broker on its performance.

- Check the broker's record. Don't assume that because he or she works for a reputable bank or other institution that the broker is competent or ethical.

- Do not buy investments over the phone. Be suspicious if you are "cold called" by someone who offers you an unbelievable deal. The chances are good that it is.

- Demand a written prospectus. If you are unable to interpret it, insist upon an explanation. Also be very wary of oral representations which are not contained in the prospectus or which appear to contradict the prospectus. The courts are likely to rule that you are bound by the written document and you cannot rely upon oral statements.

- Be sure to ask about the commissions and fees that are to be paid to the broker to determine not only the amount, but whether they are "front loaded" or "back loaded." It is the practice of some unscrupulous brokers to collect a 3 percent sales commission on the original purchase of an emerging growth fund, wait six months, and then call the client and suggest that the time has come to get out of a growth and income fund. There is usually little resistance to such recommendation, since the client doesn't have to pay any up-front charges for the switch. But the broker collects a 4 percent commission immediately, which hits the consumer when he sells the fund at a later time.

- Be sure you understand the language of the financial world. For example, when a banker tells you that what you're investing in has a *fluctuating net asset value,* hold your wallet with a little tighter grip because this means that your money is at risk!

- Don't be fooled by the name of the investment, whether it carries the logo of your bank or the words "government" or "federal." Appearances are usually deceiving.

- Write to the Securities and Exchange Commission (SEC) for introductory information about Mutual Funds, and to the AARP for *Facts About Financial Planners*; and *The Five Biggest Problems "Legitimate" Investing Poses For Older Investors.*

CHAPTER SEVEN

Is There a Lawyer in the House?

The first thing we do is kill all the lawyers.
—*King Henry VI*, William Shakespeare

The great poet touched a vein of resentment that has run deep in literature and life over the centuries. But what is often overlooked when exasperation prompts us to quote Shakespeare is that his words have been taken out of context and completely misinterpreted. They are actually a tribute to lawyers, not a condemnation.

Cade, a pretender to the throne of England who falsely claims a nobility of birth, is leading a mob toward London. He promises his inflamed followers an array of bogus reforms and benefits once he becomes king. One of his supporters, Dick Butcher, proposes to execute all the lawyers, not because they constitute a pox on English society, but so that Cade can continue to pander to the emotions and passions of the crowd rather than be forced to prove his claim by factual evidence. The lawyers are the ones who will expose Cade's false pretensions.

Lawyers, despite occupying the lower rungs of societal admiration, remain the keepers of the law's flame, and when they are extinguished, the rule of law—which holds back the rule of the jungle—

is certain to follow. In fact, closing the courthouse doors and elimi-
nating resort to established rules of law has been the course of conduct taken by virtually every totalitarian and fascist dictator
throughout history.

It's important to be mindful of the constructive role that lawyers
can and do play in our lives because there are individuals and groups
who are ever alert to seek to exploit our resentments toward the legal
profession and earn a hefty profit in the process. The elderly, again,
become the brigands' prime targets of opportunity because they have
pinched pennies and accumulated dollars and their thoughts are likely to be turning to ways in which they can pass on their treasures,
however modest, to their heirs.

If, as we are told, the only sure things in life are death and taxes,
then it's fair to ask if we can't at least beat back the tax collectors from
the grave site and not have to pay lawyers to tell us how to do it?

The answer is that it's perfectly legitimate to try to reduce, indeed
eliminate, taxes through an estate plan and to pursue this goal without the advice or services of an attorney.

But there are risks involved in doing so, especially if the effort is
made at the behest of a non-professional. If the plan is not carefully
crafted, then the prospects are high that your pockets will have been
picked by a huckster and the tax collector's cup will continue to run-
neth over—only you will not be around to feel the pain or shame at
having been duped.

There has been a recent surge in the popularity of "Living Trusts"
that warrant great scrutiny. A trust is a legal device whereby a
"grantor" or "settlor" transfers title to his or her assets to a trustee
who manages them for the benefit of selected "beneficiaries." A living trust is executed while the grantor is alive and, ordinarily, the
trust is revocable at any time by the grantor who often serves as the
trustee. The grantor can, of course, make the trust irrevocable or
designate a third party, institution, or corporation to serve in the
capacity of trustee.

One of the principal benefits of such a trust is that it avoids the probate of one's estate, which, depending upon its size and complexity, can prove time-consuming and expensive. It also protects the confidentiality of its provisions from the glare of public scrutiny.

While living trusts can be a desirable estate planning mechanism, they should be carefully prepared and reviewed by an attorney or other professional who is familiar with laws of the state where the grantor lives. What should be avoided is the temptation to sign a preprinted form that has been mass-produced by a group or organization that exaggerates the costs of hiring an attorney and promises major tax savings if you'll just sign on the bottom line.

It should be obvious that "one size" rarely fits all financial needs, and a form that may comply with, say the laws of Nevada, may be null and void in New Jersey. Moreover, the charge for joining as a member of an association that is marketing the living trust is likely to far exceed the costs of securing the services of an attorney or those associated with probating one's estate. Nonetheless, a number of national and state-based companies have been successful in targeting senior citizens and preying upon their fears by sending around door-to-door salesmen who engage in high-pressure and deceptive practices to market association memberships that include the preparation of living trusts as one of the association's many benefits.

The approach taken by these organizations is quite uniform and predictable: A well-dressed individual or couple will appear at the door and proceed with a well-rehearsed sales pitch that exaggerates the tax liability of the resident and the costs of probate and legal services. They will offer memberships in associations that have names similar to well-known, legitimate non-profit organizations, such as the American Association of Retired People (AARP), and imply that they have a connection with or endorsement by legitimate providers of aging services. Here is a classic case where you should heed the warning: *Caveat Emptor—let the buyer beware.*

Studies of older consumers have shown that, compared to younger people, elder sales prospects tend to be more trusting of salespeople, less able to recognize potential bad deals, and less knowledgeable of their consumer rights, especially those based on laws pertaining to door-to-door sales. This is no reflection on older consumers. Chances are they base their trust on the sales experiences of bygone days, when seller and buyer often knew each other and companies based their reputation on honesty. For something new and complicated, like a living trust, the older consumer has no experience to rely on and tends to defer to the expertise of the seller.

Nuel and Sylvia Stroheker of Gray, Maine, trusted their instincts *not* to trust strangers. They had cast a cold eye upon a couple who had approached them at their home one day. Mr. Stroheker said that one of the very first things that the sales team wanted to know was if they had a lawyer in the family. They did not. The sales offer stated that if the Strohekers were to join the American Association of Senior Citizens (AASC), for a cost of $1,995, they would save about $67,000. The Strohekers thought that "they were nice people and sounded good," but when they indicated that they wanted to talk to their tax consultant, the couple advised them "not to do it."

Red flags went up and warning bells and whistles went off. They called their tax consultant who proceeded to shoot holes in the slick presentation.

Similarly, when a sales representative contacted a likely prospect named Charles Barnard, the salesman did not realize he was going to make a pitch to the travel editor of AARP's *Modern Maturity*. Barnard, well aware of pitches to older consumers, thwarted the salesman's overtures, including an attempt to poke into Barnard's personal finances. When Barnard asked for information about the salesman's company, he got none.

"We don't do that," the salesman said. "You see, you're in our computer now, but if you don't make an application today, your name will come out of the computer, and that's that. We can only make house calls like this once."

When Barnard persisted, the salesman said, "I'll tell you something. We've learned something about seniors. They collect brochures. They'll take anything you give 'em for free. We don't do that. We protect people right up front."

Nor would the salesman provide a sample contract. He said he did not have a business card with his name and telephone number. He finally scrawled an 800 number on a piece of paper.

In another encounter reported by AARP, a member in Ohio was visited by a sales agent who claimed "we don't get anything" out of the transaction, implying that all the money he collected would go to the organization the AARP member was being asked to join. When the AARP member said he needed more time to decide, the agent left no literature and said he was so busy he might not be able to get back at all. This was a classic pay-now ploy used by fly-by-night operators.

But not everyone is as wary as the Strohekers, Barnard, and the Ohio question-asker.

At least seventeen people in the state of Washington alone have filed claims against the AASC; the claims total $34,000. In addition, the state has sued the company for deceptive sales practices for having offered "free" living trusts that actually cost the consumers an enrollment fee that ranged from $995 to $5,995, depending upon the person's assets, plus a $30 monthly membership charge.

AASC is not the only organization selling living trusts door-to-door. At least eight lawsuits since 1992 have been filed against other companies by the attorneys general in Iowa, North Dakota, Wisconsin, Nebraska, and Kansas.

And one should be mindful that it is not necessary for scam artists to be associated with any organization. Mrs. Marcella Patrick of Springfield, Illinois, discovered this while she was waiting in line to make a telephone call at her local bank. A lady, who professed frustration at not being able to make contact with her husband because he was always on the phone helping other people with their finances, inquired as to whether Mrs. Patrick had anyone assisting her. Mrs. Patrick suspected no ulterior motive, and indicated that she had no one advising her on financial matters and gave the woman her home phone number.

That evening the woman's husband called and paid Mrs. Patrick a visit. He stayed for three hours and, during the course of the evening, counseled her to make an investment with the $45,000 proceeds from the pending sale of her home. She paid him for what she believed was an investment from which she would receive interest payments.

When her daughter later explained that Mrs. Patrick had actually created a living trust—which she did not want—she called the man and demanded her money back. He refused to make any restitution. Fortunately, with the intervention of the Senior Citizen's Division of the Illinois Attorney General's Office, Mrs. Patrick was able to have the $1,195 returned to her.

Executing a living trust may prove to be an entirely appropriate way for seniors to handle their estate planning needs, just as following the instructions in publications such as *How to Avoid Probate* can reduce estate expenses.

Dos and Don'ts

- If you are concerned about estate taxes, wish to avoid the prospect of guardianship, or desire to maintain the confidentiality of the disposition of your assets upon death, consult an attorney or professional estate planner.

- Consider giving a family member or friend a power of attorney as a possible alternative to creating a living trust.

- Do not confide in strangers or those who do not have a connection to your community.

- If a salesman representing a company or association makes an unsolicited appearance in person or by mail or telephone, ask for written materials about the company or association, what taxes would be paid without a living trust, and the amount of attorney fees that would be involved in the planning and probate of your estate. A refusal to provide such written documentation should be a clear indication as to the unreliability of the association or company.

- Do not sign any preprinted forms that purport to create a living trust. Remember, a size 9 shoe will not serve you well if you wear size 12 or size 7.

- Ask the salesman who prepared the form and in what state it was drafted. Ask for written assurances that the documents fully comply with the laws of the state where you reside.

- If you decide to execute a living trust that has not been prepared by your attorney or professional estate planner, be sure that you do in fact transfer your assets to the trust. Otherwise, a court is likely to nullify the trust, and you will have paid a large fee for a worthless document.

- If you have been victimized by an individual or company representative as a result of misleading information or deceptive sales practices, contact the consumer division of your state's Attorney General's Office immediately.

- Contact your local bar association for information pertaining to the cost of preparing a living trust, drafting an estate plan, or probating an estate.

- For more information on living trusts, write to the American Bar Association, Governmental Affairs Office, 1800 M Street NW, Washington, D.C. 20036.

CHAPTER EIGHT

Behind Closed Doors

Cruelty, like every other vice, requires no motive outside itself; it only requires opportunity.

—*George Eliot*

Simone de Beauvoir, in her classic *The Coming of Age*, noted, "Nothing should be more expected than old age and nothing is more unforeseen." We witness the passages of our parents and grandparents, but either cannot or will not see ourselves in their place. The cleavage between knowledge and thought remains until the time arrives when the unthinkable has become the inevitable.

Doubtlessly, few of the more than 1 million elderly who currently reside in nursing homes contemplated that they would spend their final years there. Every survey reveals the obvious: Most people desire to remain in their homes, surrounded by family, friends, and familiar objects that they have accumulated over the years. The notion of being placed in an institutional setting with limited private space and cared for by professional personnel is wholly alien to the very core of our lifelong quest and need for self-reliance and independence.

But age—or a tragic accident or illness—may rob us of our physical abilities to the point where we, or those who love us, can no longer manage essential daily activities without professional assistance. Family and friends may no longer be alive or living nearby to lend a loving and caring hand that can help sustain self-sufficiency. Institutional living then becomes the only means of assuring our safety and dignity until we pass from this life into the next.

During the 1960s and early 1970s, the nursing home industry did not earn or deserve high praise. Indeed, many were considered to be inhospitable "warehouses for the dying" that provided paltry food and heavy medication, prolonging life but doing nothing to enhance or dignify it.

In the mid-1970s Congress issued a scathing indictment of the quality of nursing home care throughout the United States. Among the abuses that congressional investigations found were nursing homes that were fire traps, negligence of residents (at times leading to injury or death), unsanitary conditions, poor food preparation and handling, misappropriation and theft of the residents' possessions, inadequate control and overuse of dangerous prescription drugs, assaults on human dignity, untrained and unsupervised staff caring for nursing home residents, and profiteering by nursing home operators.

These conditions prompted the then-chairman of the Senate Subcommittee on Long-Term Care to characterize the fate of growing old and being confined to a nursing home as a "wasteland, or T.S. Eliot's rats walking on broken glass. It's the nowhere in-between this life and the great beyond. It is being robbed of your eyesight, your mobility, and even your human dignity."

The nursing home scandals of a few decades ago provided the basis for protections that are now available to nursing home residents who are covered by Medicaid or Medicare.

Nursing Home Bill of Rights

Residents of nursing homes are now protected by a Bill of Rights that includes:

- The right to choose a personal attending physician and to be fully informed about care and treatment and to participate in planning care and treatment.
- The right to be free from physical or mental abuse, corporal punishment, involuntary seclusion, and any physical or chemical restraint imposed for purposes of discipline or convenience and not required to treat the resident's medical symptoms.
- Psychopharmacologic drugs may be administered only on orders of a physician and only as part of a plan designed to eliminate or modify symptoms for which the drugs are prescribed.
- The right to privacy.
- The right to confidentiality of personal and clinical records.
- The right to reside and receive services with reasonable accommodation of individual needs and preferences and to receive notice before the room or roommate of the resident is changed.
- The right to voice grievances about treatment or care and the right to prompt effort by the facility to resolve grievances.
- The right to organize and participate in resident groups in the facility and the right of the resident's family to meet in the facility with the families of other residents.
- The right to participate in social, religious, and community activities.
- The right to examine, upon reasonable request, the results of the most recent survey of the facility and any plan in effect to correct deficiencies.
- Any other right established by the Secretary of Health and Human Services (HHS).

These are important rights that have been fought for by nursing home patients and their families and codified by law. Most nursing homes faithfully abide by them. Today the quality of care provided by the overwhelming majority of nursing homes is superb. They are staffed by highly trained nurses and professionals who provide therapy, daily exercise, and nutritious meals. Group activities are organized to instill a sense of community and educational programs offered to stimulate intellectual curiosity and creativity.

Beware of Care Givers

While the exposés of the past—and the laws inspired by those exposés—greatly improved the circumstances for nursing home residents, no profession or institution has achieved a state of perfection, and none is without its bandits and bad seeds. Nursing homes are no exception. While tremendous progress has been made throughout the industry, there are still too many reported cases of patient abuse. For example:

In Arizona, the attorney general indicted a nurse's aide for taking a resident's blank checks, forging the resident's name, and passing them at a local bank.

In another Arizona case, two care givers for the elderly (who ranged in age from 62 to 102) were convicted and sentenced to thirteen-and-a-half years in prison for aggravated assault that included karate-kicking a resident in the chest and head, spitting on and verbally abusing residents, and sexually abusing an elderly male resident. These acts were committed while the "care givers" laughed in amusement and bragged to their friends.

In Colorado, a certified nurse's aide was convicted of sexually abusing a physically helpless and mentally ill 18-year-old resident who was suffering from extreme seizure disorders.

In Indiana, a certified nurse's aide was charged with battery for abusing a resident by stuffing a fuzzy pad into her mouth in an effort to quiet her. Another Indiana facility employed an aide who was charged with sexually abusing four female residents who ranged in age from 66 to 64. Two of the victims were blind, one was mentally retarded, and the other suffered from dementia.

Also in Indiana, the former manager of a community care center confessed to stealing over $7,600 of residents' personal funds and manipulating the records to cover the theft. Not only did he manipulate the fund accounts of the residents, he also intercepted and cashed their Social Security, Railroad Retirement, Medicare, and pension checks.

In Delaware, a nurse's aide was convicted of emotionally abusing an 85-year-old resident who had died before the case went to trial. The aide tormented the resident by verbally taunting her, splashing water from a cup onto her while making spitting sounds, and placing a pot of artificial flowers on the resident's head. When the resident began to yell at the abuse, the aide told her "to kiss [my] butt," then pulled up the skirt of her uniform, shook her bottom at the resident, and placed it on the meal tray of the resident's wheelchair.

The above cases are merely illustrative of the types of abuses that can and do occur. They are exceptions to the high standards that most nursing homes maintain, but constant vigilance is required to assure that the exceptions never become the general rule.

The emotional strain of placing a parent, spouse, or other loved one in a nursing home or other type of care away from home is often tormenting enough, even without the mental anguish and fear that they will not be treated well behind closed doors. Fortunately, there are now many means by which nursing home residents and their families can have confidence about the facility they are choosing and can report suspected cases of abuse or neglect. In 1995, for example, new regulations governing inspections and certification of nursing homes went into effect, providing tougher sanctions for nursing homes that do not meet quality standards.

Understandably, families are often reluctant to report their suspicions of abuse because they fear that there may be no other place available to send their loved one who needs care, or because they believe that the patient is left to the tender or not-so-tender mercies of the nursing home's management. Retribution, subtle or otherwise, may be the reaction to your complaint. But neither you nor your loved one (or the taxpayers who fund Medicare or Medicaid) are paying to live in a house of horror. If fear is to be experienced, it should grip the hearts of those who should be stripped of their positions of trust and fitted with the garments worn by felons.

It is also important to remember that no state can claim immunity from the heinous acts of a few. What is encouraging is the dedication on the part of the nursing home industry and the state Attorneys General Offices to expose and prosecute those sick and twisted individuals who have no compunction about exploiting the most vulnerable and helpless members of our society.

Nursing Home Checklist

While even the very best nursing homes can hire a malicious or maladjusted employee who poses as a "care giver," here are some things to look for in selecting the best institutions for a loved one:

- Gather information from other families that have used the nursing home. You should be able to get such references from the nursing home itself. Ask particularly about the quality of treatment, including respect for residents' dignity and privacy.
- Inspect the home, just as you would inspect a home you were going to rent or buy. You know how clean a kitchen is supposed to be, how clean rooms should be. Use your own judgment about what you see.
- Learn about day-to-day life in the home. What activities—both individual and group—are available to residents?

- Ask to see menus and determine whether a nutritionist is either on staff or is called upon regularly to advise the home.
- Find out if physical restraints are used and what the home's policy on restraints is. (According to a study made of the effects of federal nursing home regulations, use of physical restraints/substantially decreased while humane behavior-management programs/increased.)
- Find out whether residents have access to an ombudsman for assistance when problems arise.
- Learn the home's policy on participation in decisionmaking. If a resident is competent to make decisions, is she or he allowed to participate in decision-making? Is the resident given advance notice, in writing, of any changes in daily routine?
- Make sure that the nursing home provides for individualized needs and does a credible assessment of each resident. If you detect a "ward" mentality, try another home.
- Ask for a plan of care, with specific goals, methods, and ways of appraising those goals and methods.
- Determine the staffing of licensed personnel. Ideally, the home should have a guaranteed twenty-four-hour licensed nursing service.
- If there is need for psychiatric care, make sure that there is family participation in the therapy. And find out what role drugs play in regular care of the residents.
- Finally, ask yourself this question: Is this the best place to make your loved one—or yourself—as independent as possible, as comfortable as possible, as content as possible?

Home Health Care

In responding to the recognition that "home is where the heart is," government policies have shifted vast resources to support the delivery of health services to people who prefer to reside in their homes. In 1994, more than 7 million people received some form of home health care. Between 1990 and 1995, Medicare expenditures for home health care climbed from $3.3 billion to more than $16 billion. The current Medicaid federal share for home health care is $4.1 billion and is expected to reach approximately $18.5 billion by the year 2000. Shorter hospital stays, along with new technologies, have allowed an expanding aging population to remain at home and receive medical treatment and assistance.

While at-home health care is often desirable, not only because it is considered to be less expensive than institutional care and more compatible with the patient's wishes, it also offers fertile ground for abuse. That is because it is inadequately regulated, with multiple providers delivering services, at times with little direct supervision and monitoring of the quality of care being given.

Even with thinly stretched budgets and tight resources, state and federal agencies have taken steps to crack down on individuals and home care services companies that have engaged in fraudulent billing schemes, including overbilling for services rendered, grossly inflating the number of hours their employees have worked, and billing for services rendered to people who have already died or never existed. More importantly, a number of cases have involved companies that have recklessly sent untrained, unqualified, and unlicensed aides into the private homes of thousands of critically ill and care-dependent patients.

In New York, for example, the owner of an at-home health care agency was sentenced to serve three to nine years in prison (and the firm's billing clerk was sentenced to one to three years) for perpetrating a scheme to fraudulently bill the state for more than $1 million for nursing services rendered to home-bound Medicaid patients by unlicensed and largely untrained aides, some of whom were illegal immigrants. Not only do schemes like this defraud Medicaid and taxpayers out of millions of dollars, they also pose the risk that unsupervised and untrained individuals will financially exploit those they serve.

In Maine, a certified nurse's aide was sentenced to serve three years in jail, with all but thirty days suspended, and four years on probation for adding her name to a patient's credit cards and charging more than $7,000 for purchases that she made. Just as there are abusive misfits who make their way onto the staffs of nursing homes, we can anticipate that they are likely to seek payroll opportunities with home care agencies and firms.

The role of home health care is likely to grow dramatically in the future. When properly administered, it is a sound and economical component of our health care system. But because of the billions of dollars expended for home-care services and a weak regulatory mechanism over the industry itself, government agencies, physicians, nurses, trade associations, relatives, and friends of those who receive home health care will have to exercise a higher level of scrutiny and oversight if abuses of the system are to be deterred and contained.

Violence Against Elderly

In addition to being on guard against abuse and neglect of older Americans that could occur in long-term care facilities, such as nursing homes, and in home care, there is another dimension of elder abuse that is on the rise: abuse of the elderly within their own families.

Violence is an epidemic that has reached staggering proportions in this country. The 1980s arguably were the most violent decade of the century, if not in U.S. history, and the 1990s threaten even to top this record. On an average day, physical violence kills sixty-five people and injures 6,000 more. This is more than twice the casualty rate that our nation sustained at the height of the Vietnam war. In fact, in the last five years, we have lost more Americans to violence than we lost in Korea and Vietnam combined.

None of us is immune from this epidemic. Violence knows no geographic, age, ethnic, or economic boundaries. It is not confined to only the bad neighborhoods or the poor side of town, but reaches the homes of the wealthy and the famous. Sadly, in the United States, family violence is one of the most prevalent forms of violence sweeping our nation. Family violence has become as common as giving birth: There are about 4 million instances of each annually in the United States.

Physical, sexual, and emotional abuse within the family shatters the lives of millions of children each year, inflicting deep wounds of distrust and anger that take a lifetime to heal. Once more, family violence often results in a cycle of violence for generations, when abused children grow up and apply the only parenting skills that they know.

Violence takes a particularly heavy toll against women in our society, including women in midlife and older women. Crime and fear of violence makes prisoners of many women as they age. They are afraid to leave their homes, afraid to walk their neighborhood streets, or to go shopping. More than 1 million older American women are victims of violence each year. Shockingly, twice as many women over the age of 65 are mugged at or near their homes than younger women—and three in four of these incidents occur in broad daylight. Fear of crime causes countless older women to curtail their activities at the very same time in their lives that it is vital to stay active and involved for their own physical and psychological well-being.

For many older women, staying home does not shield them from violence. According to a 1994 report of the Older Women's League, in 1993 more than 700,000 women between the ages of 45 and 65 were physically abused by their spouses. In 1991, 40 percent of the violent crimes against women age 65 or older were committed by family members, friends, or acquaintances.

The compelling case of "Florence," who came before a congressional committee to share the story of her own years of abuse, vividly illustrates how women in our very own communities live with the secret horror of family violence. Florence told her story this way:

"I was married to an alcoholic for forty-four years. We had three daughters. He was a loving father. We spent every summer boating and camping. But then the drinking started and it escalated. The abuse began. When he drank, he became a monster; but only with me, not with the girls. But, of course, they suffered mental abuse."

"After they left home, things got really bad. I had two broken wrists, cracked ribs, was held down with his knee on my chest with a knife at my throat. I was made to crawl across the floor with a gun resting on my head, ready to fire. I've been choked until I was limp, and then he would drop me on the floor with a kick. I've been spit on, thrown through a window, dragged into the lake as he said he was going to drown me. Fortunately, he was always so drunk that I got away from him."

"For the last two years of his life, I never changed into night-clothes, as I knew he would chase me out of the house with a gun. I have spent the night in churches, old cars, sheds, or crouched under a tree, waiting for him to sober up. Sometimes I would go to a motel if I had enough money. This went on for many nights. The last time he chased me out, he shot at my car as I left the yard. I went to a motel. I thought it was safe to go home the next morning, but when I got there he was still drunk. He knocked my glasses off and punched me in the stomach. While he was in the bathroom, I grabbed my pocketbook and glasses and ran across the field to a neighbor's."

To escape her terror, Florence went to a shelter for abused women. Meanwhile, her husband continued to comb the streets to find her. After three days of fruitless searching, he hooked a hose to his car and committed suicide. Florence, who was 64 years old at the time of her husband's suicide, testified that all she could say was "Thank God it's over."

Florence's case is not unique. Thousands of older women suffer daily at the hands of their "loved ones." They are often too ashamed to come forward because they do not know where to go, because they feel trapped or isolated, or because they do not want to admit that this terror could really be happening within their very own families.

Fortunately, state legislatures have begun to recognize the extent of elder abuse and have passed laws against it. All fifty states, the District of Columbia, Guam, and the Virgin Islands have enacted some form of state law addressing elder abuse in both family and institutional settings. These fifty-three jurisdictions have placed more than seventy laws on the books to protect elderly people from abuse, neglect, or exploitation. Many of these laws also protect disabled adults from abuse or neglect. In addition to these many state laws, the federal government has enacted legislation creating programs aimed at the prevention of elder abuse as part of the Older Americans Act.

State laws on adult and elder abuse are very diverse, with some addressing abuse in institutional settings while others focus on elder abuse or neglect within the home. State laws also differ on the types of abuse covered, including physical harm, neglect, mental anguish, or financial abuse.

Many states have adopted mandatory reporting requirements for professionals from various fields when there is evidence or suspicion of elder abuse. Many states, for example, require physicians or other health professionals, social workers, police, and others working with the elderly or disabled to report cases of suspected abuse. Besides specifying who must report cases of elder abuse, many states have adopted so-called "voluntary reporters" laws that provide procedures for anyone voluntarily reporting instances of elder abuse.

In 1983, California sought to address the issue of who is responsible for elder abuse when the state created a new crime known as "elder or dependent adult abuse." The statute makes a criminal "any person who willfully causes or allows an elder to suffer, or who directly inflicts, unjustifiable pain or mental suffering on any elder...."

Under the law a woman was charged with elder abuse following the death of her partially paralyzed, 67-year-old father. Her two brothers had assumed primary responsibility for his care—and supplemented their income with their father's pension. The woman paid frequent visits to his home. She noticed that her father's physical condition was deteriorating and that the house was in a squalid condition. Although she complained to her brothers, she took no action to correct living conditions or to secure medical assistance for her father.

Over a Thanksgiving weekend, the woman and her brothers kept their father in his room with the door closed in order to reduce the stench of his incontinence. No one bothered to check on his condition throughout the entire weekend. On the following Monday, the father was found dead. A pathologist determined that he had died of septic shock due to bed sores that, in his opinion, had been caused by malnutrition, dehydration, and neglect. The two brothers were charged with manslaughter and their sister with elder abuse.

The California statutory language is broad and sweeping, and accordingly, has invited challenge. Responding to an appeal in this case, the Supreme Court of California declared the elder abuse statute to be constitutional, but narrowed its application from any person to only those who have a special relationship to the elder. It is important to note, however, that the court did not restrict the statute's provisions to "care givers" and thereby sanctioned the imposition of a legal duty upon those where a basic moral imperative commands action rather than indifference or neglect. California's initiative is certain to prove controversial as greater attention is paid to the abuse of elders by their spouses or family members.

In Maryland, a brother and sister were arrested for leaving their 81-year-old mother unattended for a month. She was allegedly kept, nude, on a living room couch until she died of bed sores and infection from her own waste, according to Maryland officials. The law under which they were arrested and indicted prohibits the "abuse or neglect of a vulnerable person." Maryland had recently revised the law to cover people other than care givers.

It would seem unlikely that California or any other state will seek to expand the application of elder abuse to include cases involving the infliction of severe emotional distress by a spouse or impose a duty to prevent such psychological torment on family members. But if psychological terrorism is severe enough to take a physical toll upon an elder, it is not inconceivable for a court to one day find a duty on the part of those who have a "special relationship" to intervene or risk criminal consequences.

Dos and Don'ts

• If you are planning to make use of a nursing home, follow the guide mentioned in this chapter.

• Find out what local ordinances and state laws cover nursing homes in your state.

• If you believe that a resident is being exploited financially or physically abused, complain to the owner-manager of the facility. Should your complaint prove ineffective, or fruitless to lodge, contact your state's Attorney General's Office. (See Appendix 8, page 178, for a list of where to report elder abuse in your state.)

• Similarly, if you believe a neighbor or friend is being abused by a family member, check with local social welfare agencies and remind them of "elder abuse" laws on the book.

CHAPTER NINE

Rainbow's End and Other Ripoffs

Habitual intoxication is the epitome of every crime.

During the past several decades, we have witnessed a decline and fall in many of the values that we inherited from our ancestors, such as hard work, self-discipline, and individual responsibility for our actions. With the growth of governmental programs designed to support the dispossessed and less fortunate among us has come the notion of a vested entitlement to income, housing, food, health care, and happiness—without regard as to whether one is responsible for his or her status or condition.

Our capacity for compassion and charity, according to author Marvin Olasky, has been transformed into a cold corporate welfarism that has led to perpetuation of an undesirable state of dependency. "[W]e need to realize that we do not increase compassion by expanding it to cover everything," he wrote. "Instead, we kill a good word by making it mean too much, and nothing."

Our compassion has been especially made "to mean too much and nothing" in the programs that provide disability benefits to those who are addicted to drugs and alcohol. As of 1994, some 250,000 substance abusers were receiving roughly $1.4 billion in cash benefits from two federal programs—the Social Security Disability Program (DI) and the Supplemental Security Income (SSI) program. Only about 78,000 of these recipients—or less than a third—were required to seek treatment for their addictions or required to have someone else collect the checks on their behalf. Of the 78,000 required to seek treatment, only a small percentage ever did so. Moreover, while the law required that payments be made to a responsible third party rather than to the disabled recipient, in many cases payments were simply made to family members who either turned the money over to the recipient or purchased the drugs or alcohol for them.

The director of a drug and alcohol rehabilitation shelter in Denver, Colorado, came forward to a congressional committee to describe how egregious these abuses of taxpayer dollars are. Here is what Bob Cote told the Senate Special Committee on Aging:

> I first became aware of Supplemental Security Income about six years ago when four gentlemen were passing out pamphlets on skid row where our facility is located in Denver, Colorado, putting them in the hands of these street drunks. I went out there out of curiosity and got one. It said, "Are you an alcoholic or a drug addict? Then you may qualify for Supplemental Security Income up to $425 a month." At that time, that's what they were getting. . . .
>
> A bar two doors down from my facility was the recipient of $160,000 in SSI checks. A liquor store three blocks down from me was the recipient of over $200,000 in SSI checks. They were sending them as a mailing address and they were running up tabs. It's suicide on the installment plan—is what SSI stands for.

In other cases of abuse, lump-sum retroactive cash payments for disability in amounts up to $25,000 were being paid directly to addicts who proceeded to overdose on drugs or kill themselves or others while driving under the influence.

Every American citizen should be outraged by compassion run amok, but senior citizens should be particularly concerned because, once again, the Social Security trust funds are being drained away to support those who have shown little regard for self-responsibility.

It may be impossible to prevent some individuals from finding their rainbow at the end of a needle or the bottom of a bottle, but those individuals should not be able to insist that other members of society pay taxes from their hard labor to support their dysfunction. Fortunately, the law was changed in 1994 to mandate rehabilitative treatment for those claiming disability due to substance abuse. The law also requires a termination of benefits after a period of three years. More changes are certain to come to the disability programs as we as a society return to the sterner virtues of individual responsibility and accountability that has provided the bedrock of America's greatness.

The SSI program, created to alleviate the deprivations of the most disadvantaged among us, has attracted other forms of abuse. Predators now stalk it as they would a weak and defenseless victim.

In 1993, the SSI rolls embraced 6 million Americans who received $20 billion in benefits. Just eight years earlier, in 1985, there were 4.1 million SSI recipients, with federal payments totaling $8.8 billion. Of the 6 million SSI recipients, 4.4 million were classified as disabled— more than half of whom were mentally disabled. The mentally disabled, in fact, represent the fastest growing segment of the SSI program, accounting for 55 percent of disability payments, which reflects an increase of 25 percent since 1975.

Members of another rapidly expanding aspect of the SSI program are the immigrants who qualify for benefits. In 1993, more than 683,000 immigrants received benefits, representing a 50 percent increase in just a four-year period.

There is little doubt that mental illness is a disabling condition. It rests like a dark shadow on the brain, blocking out light, distorting beauty, inspiration, and the soul-soothing pleasures that are divinely bestowed upon us. If the shadow is deep and dark enough, it will sever and disconnect the lines that run to the very core of our being, interrupting our ability to function as a constructive and contributing member of society.

We recognize it as a disease, one that for many is treatable and for others an irreparable affliction—and for all compensable. But surely our suspicions are arroused when we see such a dramatic surge in recent years in the disabled status of the immigrants who reach our shores.

Investigations reveal that a new growth industry has emerged among the immigrant and refugee communities. These are so-called "middlemen" who assist clients in a wide variety of services, including applying for SSI benefits and other welfare programs. Some of the services provided by the middlemen are legal, while other services, which also involve corrupt physicians and lawyers, are clearly fraudulent.

Middlemen typically charge their clients between $2,500 and $3,000 to apply for SSI benefits. The clients have to pay an up-front fee and make periodic payments until the benefits are awarded. Frequently, the middlemen will obtain their final payments from the clients' first disability checks.

Since many of the immigrants applying for welfare assistance have at best a limited ability to speak English, the all-purpose middlemen serve as translators as well. To insure that the clients receive whatever benefit is being sought, the middlemen coach them on precisely what needs to be said—including how to feign some form of mental impairment, such as depression or delayed stress syndrome.

One scheme targeted for exposure by California officials involved a clinic that serviced a Southeast Asian community. A middleman took an undercover operative along with a group of two dozen "patients" to visit the same doctor one evening at 7 o'clock. While awaiting consultation with the doctor, the other patients laughed and joked about how easy it was to bilk the system and live off the "free money for life."

The middleman had coached each of them how to complain of "headaches, nightmares, poor appetites, and depression. These are symptoms, which cannot be medically disproved, and will qualify as some form of mental impairment."

The state's undercover operative remained silent while the middleman communicated his clients' "problems" to the doctor during a five-minute session. This quicky visit blossomed into a billing statement that represented six hours of service—two hours for testing, two hours for reviewing the tests, and two hours for writing the report. The sum total billed by the doctor for the two dozen patients was $10,000, a tidy sum for about an hour's work.

California investigators hired a psychologist to evaluate 300 SSI files seized from a clinic. All 300 patients had been diagnosed by the clinic doctor as being "mildly mentally retarded." The investigators' psychologist reported that all 300 files had a "numbing sameness to them." And all the files omitted the patient's work history, even though this is a requirement when applying for SSI eligibility. The investigators also discovered that of the 5,897 individuals brought to the clinic by suspected middlemen, 3,470 had applied for SSI and 1,981 had been granted benefits. The rest were awaiting approval or were in the appeals process. By the time the investigation was conducted, the 1,981 successful applicants had received nearly $39 million in SSI benefits.

Of course, more than doctors' fraudulent fees are involved. Most of the "disabled patients" are likely to receive either SSI or DI benefits for the rest of their lives.

The Social Security Administration (SSA) is required to conduct periodic reviews of those receiving DI payments to determine whether there has been any medical improvement in the recipient's condition. But this oversight function is in a state of paralytic shock. SSA performed only 49,000 of the required reviews of the DI cases, which now number in excess of l.2 million. And in 1993, the SSA had *no* SSI cases under review. (It is not mandated to do so.)

As a result of this lack of reviews, Social Security trust funds are calculated to lose $1.4 billion by the end of 1997 in unnecessary payments to those whose medical condition warrants termination from the program. Equally ominous is the enormity of the wave of disability applicants rushing toward the SSA's doors: More than 700,000 applications for SSI and DI benefits are pending, along with 350,000 petitioners awaiting appeal from initial denial of benefits.

Many of fraudulent schemes, such as those just described, involve a broad range of ethnic groups, including Armenians, Ukrainians, Russians, Vietnamese, Iranians, Chinese, and Cambodians. Determining who among them is truly entitled to our compassion and dollars is going to prove taxing. Indeed.

Subsidized Housing Scams

Fraudulent and abusive schemes that siphon away tax dollars are certainly not confined to the Social Security Disability Program. The federal housing programs provide another opportunity ripe for those who want to make a fast buck at the expense of taxpayers. Since the Great Society days of Lyndon B. Johnson, Americans have made a determined effort to provide decent and affordable housing for low-income citizens. A vast array of programs are offered through the Departments of Housing and Urban Development (HUD), Veterans Affairs (VA), and Agriculture.

Once again, we find increasing evidence of white-collar vandals who exhibit no moral qualms in robbing both Peter and Paul of their dreams of a decent life. And with the predation come frauds that drain federal money from senior citizens.

Ordinarily, a developer of a low-income, multifamily housing project will obtain a bank loan that is insured by a federal agency. The rental income generated by the tenants (which may be subsidized by the government) should be sufficient to pay the owner/manager fees, the proper maintenance of the facility, and the principal and interest on the bank loan.

Equity skimming (actually a misnomer since the owner has little equity committed) occurs when the owner of the project uses or diverts the money received for his or her personal interests or pleasures rather than pay the mortgage or maintenance and upkeep fees. This diversion of funds results in a default on the mortgage, forcing the federal agency to pay off the bank loan and assume responsibility for the project. Often the owner of the project remains in place, making payments to the federal agency instead of a bank. Regrettably, the diversion schemes frequently continue, causing the project to fall into a state of disrepair while forcing the tenants to endure intolerable living conditions.

A recent case in New York involved a nursing home operator who made cash distributions of more than $560,000 to partners. In addition, the operator received $1.7 million in management and consulting fees that could not be verified as reasonable. Finally, the operator paid more than $273,000 in costs never approved by the federal insuring agency. While the partners in this particular operation were living high, the nursing home residents were living below what the state of New York found acceptable.

This is not an unusual example of abuse. A replication of this activity has been discovered in a number of states. The inspector general of HUD estimates that equity skimming has cost the taxpayers nearly $6 billion to date. HUD has approximately 20,000 projects in its insured mortgage portfolio, whose value totals more than $40 billion. The agency holds another $10 billion in defaulted mortgages. An additional $10 billion worth of HUD-insured mortgages is estimated to be at risk of default. In 1993 alone HUD paid to private banks $965 million in multi-family housing mortgage insurance claims.

While not all of these insured mortgages are in default due to equity skimming, the practice has become sufficiently endemic to warrant intense scrutiny and severe punishment. In another case involving contract fraud, the owners of a New York company, a married couple, received $23 million in government-funded contracts to perform work for the New York Housing Authority. According to a HUD inspector general report, the owners formed a "shell" company that "inflated costs, skimmed funds as consultant fees," and rerouted other money intended to be spent on improving the housing. Instead, the owners diverted a portion of the funds to buy a horse farm in Florida. The couple was convicted, sentenced to eight-year prison terms, and fined $22,000.

Food Stamp Fraud

Unscrupulous entrepreneurs have still another path toward illegal riches: Uncle Sam's food stamp program.

A common fraud involves illegal trafficking in food stamps. In these schemes, the food stamps usually change hands several times before they are redeemed. A drug dealer, for example, sells $10 worth of crack cocaine for $30 in food stamps. The dealer then uses $200 in food stamps to buy a gun with a street value of $100. The gun dealer in turn sells the $200 in food stamps for $125 to the operator of a small store who is not authorized to accept food stamps. That store owner then sells the $200 in food stamps for $150 to a grocer who *is* authorized to redeem them. The food stamps finally end their long journey by being redeemed by the grocer through the Department of Agriculture—for their full face value of $200.

Investigations have discovered that food stamp schemes such as these are pervasive throughout the nation. In Ohio, for example, state and federal agents who raided more than fifty grocery stores found dusty canned goods, long-expired cans of infant formula, and refrigerators containing months-old meat—all part of the disguise for a massive food stamp fraud.

The investigation uncovered several so-called "shell" stores which existed mostly for the purpose of buying food stamps from the poor and redeeming them for huge profits. In one Cleveland store, investigators discovered a store that processed $500,000 in food stamps a year, even though on its shelves were little more than beer and wine (which cannot be legally purchased with food stamps) and snacks, such as potato chips.

These vignettes provide just a tiny glimpse of ways that contractors, middlemen, and other cunning participants in federal programs have found ways to beat the system and line their own pockets. As with so many other cases of fraudulent schemes, society suffers a double blow: first to the taxpayers who provide the sweat, labor, and dollars for the programs; then to the desperate, deserving recipients who are deprived of our best intentions.

Dos (for Legislators)

Most people cannot directly do much about fraud involving Supplemental Security Income, the Social Security Disability Program, federal housing programs, and food stamps. But you can support legislators grappling with these frauds. In letters to your congressional representatives and senators, tell them your feelings about some of the proposed reforms to wipe out fraud and put these programs back on the track that Congress set up for them. Here are some of the reform ideas contemplated by lawmakers.

• Require approved translators for SSI applicants or recipients who need translation. Do not rely on translators who are part of the fraud package. Establish a quality-assurance program that insures that translations are accurate and complete.

- Require solid "recipient identifying information" as a way of cutting back on fraud. With such data, there is a better chance of tracking second- or third-time offenders.

- Speed up the process that puts possible cases of fraud before the U.S. attorney general or an equivalent state prosecutor.

- Reopen SSI cases where fraud is suspected.

- Give the Social Security Administration the power to impose civil penalties against "middlemen," their medical confederates, and SSI recipients who engage in fraudulent schemes designed to enroll ineligible individuals in the SSI program.

- Pursue collection of prior SSI payments from SSI recipients whose benefits are terminated because the benefits were obtained fraudulently.

CHAPTER TEN

HMOs: Back to the Future?

_____

The voice of great events is proclaiming to us, Reform, that
you may preserve.

— *Thomas Babington Macaulay*

In the spring of 1995, the trustees of the Medicare Trust Fund
issued a stark warning: Medicare Part A (which pays hospital bills)
is sliding speedily toward insolvency. Beginning in 1996, the payments for services rendered to Medicare beneficiaries have exceeded
the fund's revenues, the first time for such an occurrence since the
creation of Medicare itself.

The stream of red ink will gather momentum, swell into a flood,
and overrun its protective banks by the year 2002. The reason for
this turn of fortune can be found not in the stars, but in the numbers. In 1965, there were 5.6 taxpayers to each Medicare beneficiary. Today there are 3.3 to each, and by the year 2002, there will be
only 3.1 taxpayers for each beneficiary. Extrapolate to the year
2035 and we find the ratio to be 2 taxpayers to every person drawing benefits.

The mathematics march relentlessly to the conclusion that
Medicare is going bankrupt because more is being spent on retirees

than they have contributed to the Fund. A couple who retires in 1995 with one worker, for example, will collect, on average, $126,700 more in Medicare benefits than they contributed during their working years. A two-worker couple will, on average, collect $117,200 more than they contributed.

Clearly, it's imperative to take corrective action now to protect the financial integrity of Medicare and preserve it for future generations. But exactly what is to be done? Raise taxes to meet the Medicare expenditures that are increasing at the rate of 10 percent each year? The Medicare trustees suggest that the exercise of this option would require a 44 percent increase in payroll taxes. Another alternative would be to reduce benefits by 30 percent. Or some combination of benefit cuts and tax increases possibly could be constructed to restore solvency.

Assuming it were economically desirable and politically possible to impose a significant increase in payroll taxes, the flow of red ink would be stanched only temporarily. Because Medicare expenditures continue to grow 10 percent annually, it would only be a matter of a few years before the Fund would be placed on an emergency life-support system.

A System Full of Leaks and Holes

To define the challenge differently, consider if the heating bills for our homes were increasing each year to the point where the payments were exceeding our income. And assume that there were holes in the roof, the walls were not insulated, and several windows were broken so that a substantial amount of heat was being wasted.

We could attempt to keep the house warm by increasing our income to purchase additional fuel. Of course, we might not be able to obtain a raise from our boss or secure a second or third job in order to increase our income. But assuming that we could do so, the futility of attempting to satisfy our thermal needs in an uninsulated and drafty home is clear.

The wiser choice would be to make structural repairs to the home so as to limit the amount of fuel consumed. Conservation in this context is the key to satisfying our physical needs and financial abilities.

Does the analogy apply to our health care needs? If it does, what kind of structural repairs can we make that will conserve our resources, maximize efficiency, and not compromise quality?

Controlling Costs

There is little question that reductions in the growth of the Medicare program will have to be made if it is to be saved. Curbing the annual increases in costs means either of two possibilities: Doctors and hospitals will have to receive less money for their services (this has already occurred, resulting in the shifting of costs to those who are covered by private insurance plans, such as Blue Cross/Blue Shield), or beneficiaries will have to absorb more of the copayments and deductibles than they currently do. The latter alternative will pose a serious financial challenge to those of limited resources. So it is likely that any increased costs imposed on beneficiaries will be based on one's ability to pay—"means tested."

But assuming that a reduction in cost growth can be structured, it solves the problem only temporarily. And it does so, if we recall the previous metaphor, by adding more heating fuel to a house with gaping holes, rather than making the house more energy-efficient.

The central problem is that our current health care system provides an incentive for **over-utilization**—the more services provided by hospitals and physicians, the higher their reimbursement or income. To the extent that beneficiaries believe that they are only receiving the care for which they are fully paying (which is not the case), they are inclined to maximize the use of their entitlement.

Private organizations and companies have turned to the concept of "managed care" or Health Maintenance Organizations (HMOs) to moderate or alter the incentives for over-utilization. While there are many varieties of managed care plans (each of which should be carefully studied), the basic concept involves providing a fixed amount of money monthly (or annually) to those doctors and hospitals who participate in the program, whether or not they actually treat the individuals who are covered by the plan. This payment method is known as "capitation." This approach has resulted in reducing the annual growth in healthcare costs by 50 percent of that experienced by Medicare.

In other words, the health plan is paid a fixed amount for treating each beneficiary, regardless of how many services they use. The health plan is then at risk for controlling costs, which it done by such means as negotiating rates with providers, emphasizing prevention, and limiting access to service. The plans themselves put pressure on the physicians to deliver "cost efficient" care. If they are perceived as "over-utilizers," they can be dropped from the plan.

It should be obvious, however, that just as the current Medicare system encourages over-utilization, managed care programs may encourage doctors and hospitals to provide less care and treatment to their patients, since the less service provided, the higher the profit retained from the fixed payments. Thus, by shifting our focus to the cutting of costs, there is the danger that we will lose our concern for, and witness the decline of, the quality of medical care itself.

Approximately 60 percent of the current workforce now participates in a form of managed care, such as HMO plans. By contrast, although 75 percent of Medicare beneficiaries live in areas served by HMOs, only 9 percent of them have opted to join HMOs.

As Congress seeks to preserve the solvency of Medicare by encouraging Medicare beneficiaries to shift to HMOs, there needs to be a careful analysis of the rewards and risks offered by managed care plans.

HMOs offer a number of attractive features to their enrollees:

- In most instances, Medicare beneficiaries who want to join a Medicare-approved HMO cannot be turned down due to pre-existing medical conditions. (There are a few exceptions to this rule, as explained in the section below on what to consider when joining an HMO). This is an advantage over some traditional health insurance policies that "cherry pick" who they will cover. In other words, some traditional health insurance plans select only the healthy for coverage and reject the ill or infirm.
- Enrollees have far less paperwork with which to contend.
- Coverage in HMOs often offer a wider range of services to their members, such as paying for prescription drugs, eye and dental care, and preventive health care, such as routine cancer screening and even exercise classes.
- Enrollees often have fewer out-of-pocket costs, since HMO plans often offer attractive coverage benefits with fewer deductibles or copayments.
- The need for Medigap or supplemental coverage is eliminated while the Medicare beneficiary is enrolled in the plan.
- There is an emphasis on primary and preventive care rather than on expensive medical procedures.

Surveys of those in the private sector who utilize HMOs disclose a high level of satisfaction with the medical care they receive. For example, the inspector general of the Department of Health and Human Services surveyed almost 3,000 Medicare beneficiaries enrolled in HMOs and found that most beneficiaries are very satisfied customers. The vast majority of those surveyed reported that their HMOs provided adequate services, that they had good access to primary, specialty, and hospital care, and that they were personally wellserved by their plan and plan doctors.

But what glitters as gold for some may turn out to be little more than polished brass for others. The General Accounting Office (GAO), in surveying Medicare beneficiaries who are enrolled in HMOs, has found some major abuses in the areas of:

- The marketing of HMO plans;
- The denial of care to patients and lengthy delays in the appeals of denied coverage, including coverage for nursing home and home health care;
- The referral of patients to specialists who were not experienced in the type of surgery or medical procedures required by the patients.

A study conducted by the Center for Health Care Rights, an independent, non-profit organization based in Los Angeles, confirms much of the findings of the GAO, and has found problems in HMOs in the areas of marketing practices, access and quality, due process rights, and lack of information on access and quality of services provided by the HMO.

There are documented cases of HMO employees or agents engaging in high-pressure tactics to enroll patients, including deception and outright fraud. (The "Tin Man" tactics described in Chapter 3 are not limited to home repair frauds.)

One elderly Los Angeles widow of limited education, for example, was paid an unsolicited visit by an HMO marketing agent. Although the agent warned her that Medicare was about to be terminated, the woman refused to drop her Medicare coverage and enroll in the HMO plan. The agent, nonetheless, persuaded her to sign an enrollment form by telling her it was simply to be used to verify the agent's visit.

Another elderly woman, who did not have any private means of transportation, and who had previously had two hip replacement surgeries, enrolled in an HMO believing that she had purchased a

Medicare supplemental policy and would continue to be treated by nearby physicians. She later discovered that the closest HMO primary care physician was 10 miles from her home in an area not served by public transportation. She was denied coverage by Medicare and is appealing the denial of her claim while seeking a retroactive disenrollment from the HMO.

A common pressure tactic employed by HMO marketers is to provide limited information about the plan's coverage and terms and then plead with the enrollees not to ask for additional information when those in the HMO office call to verify that the enrollee understands the plan. The marketers claim that this will reflect poorly on their skills and possibly jeopardize their jobs. Playing on sympathy works particularly well with older prospective customers.

The problem presented by mistaken or uninformed enrollment is a serious one. Should the beneficiaries continue to seek medical care under the fee-for-service system, they will likely have to pay expensive medical bills that both Medicare and the HMO will deny coverage of.

Although the Health Care Financing Administration (HCFA) does offer assistance to help enrollees seek retroactive disenrollment due to mistake or fraud, returning them to Medicare's fee-for-service program and voiding their HMO enrollment, beneficiaries can face weeks and months of anxiety and harassment from collection agencies demanding payment for the medical bills that are outstanding.

Another problem associated with the disenrollment process is that HMO enrollees usually discontinue their supplemental coverage upon enrollment. If they subsequently disenroll, they may discover that their insurance companies no longer will sell them supplemental policies.

Even where there is no evidence of uninformed consent or fraudulent marketing, those who choose to disenroll from an HMO simply because they are dissatisfied with the care (an option that is always available) can face the denial of the supplemental coverage they once possessed. They may have developed a medical condition while they were in the HMO that now makes them ineligible for the Medigap insurance policy.

Perhaps the most serious criticism of the managed care system is the delay in treatment or denial of approval for services the beneficiary expects to receive. In order for an HMO to function efficiently, it necessarily must exercise vigilant oversight on the types of medical procedures its participating hospitals and physicians can provide, as well as those medically necessary procedures it will cover that are beyond the scope of expertise available within the HMO's plan.

Some examples include:

- A beneficiary who suffered from recurrent urinary tract infections obtained test results that suggested the presence of prostate cancer. Several months passed before the HMO had him examined by a urologist, who then performed additional tests. The patient was rushed to a hospital emergency room and treated for undiagnosed bladder cancer that had perforated his large intestine.

- During a twenty-four hour period, a beneficiary with symptoms of pneumonia and a heart attack twice sought and was denied admission to a hospital. The HMO primary care physician concurred that admission should be denied. Following the second rejection for admission, the beneficiary died on the way to see his primary physician.

- A beneficiary's primary care physician had recommended thyroplastic surgery to repair a damaged vocal chord. The HMO group approved the procedure but referred the patient to a surgeon who had never performed this type of surgery. The HMO initially refused to approve referral to a surgeon who was not covered by its plan. Only after persistence by a

Medicare advocacy program did the HMO grant approval for an out-of-plan surgeon to perform the operation.

- A Medicare beneficiary who suffered from diabetes and circulatory difficulties due to vein blockage in his lower limbs had a partial amputation of his foot in 1994. When his problems persisted, his primary care physician recommended that the man's foot and leg be amputated just below the knee. A second medical opinion by another doctor in the same medical group supported the recommendation. The patient, however, sought an opinion from an out-of-plan physician and learned about vein bypass procedure, known as revascularization, that would save his leg provided it was done immediately. The HMO indicated that the patient could not transfer his plan to a group that offered this procedure until the end of the month—an intolerable delay under the circumstances. Intervention by California officials and a Medicare advocacy program managed to reverse the initial denial, thereby saving the patient's leg.

- An 88-year-old woman was placed in a nursing home following a stroke so that she could receive speech, physical, and occupational therapy for forty-five days. While in the nursing home, she developed a bladder infection and began vomiting intermittently throughout the day. After two weeks had passed, the woman's HMO notified her that she would no longer qualify for skilled nursing care under the HMO plan or Medicare. The woman's son had no choice but to disenroll his mother from the plan, but he was successful in having Medicare pay the expenses for the seventy-four days that she remained in the nursing home. Although the woman returned to her Medicare plan, she was unable to obtain the supplemental policy she had dropped when she enrolled with the HMO.

- A beneficiary of a risk-based New York HMO was visiting his daughter in Florida when he began to experience severe difficulty breathing. He was rushed to a hospital and had a family member notify his HMO that he was receiving treatment outside the HMO's service area. Upon his return to New York, his HMO informed him that his treatment was not covered because no one notified the HMO within forty-eight hours of the emergency. (There was no need for the beneficiary to contest the issue of timely notification because the law prevents an HMO from denying coverage to a Medicare beneficiary solely because the HMO was not notified of the out-of-plan treatment.)

The foregoing examples are meant to be illustrative of the types of problems that have occurred with various HMO plans. In spite of these difficulties, most private sector employees enrolled in managed care programs continue to express solid satisfaction with the quality of care they are receiving.

Of course, it may be that this segment of the population is generally younger and healthier than those 65 years and older and require less medical attention and treatment. But Medicare HMOs appear to be on the rise as well. In 1992, there were only 96 such HMOs covering 1.6 million people. Today, they number 165 and cover 2.6 million members, while 70 more are awaiting approval by the federal government.

Unquestionably, managed care programs, when efficiently *and* humanely operated, offer the potential for high quality and less costly care for their members. But those that are unprofessionally run or managed by those whose eyes are fixed on bottom line costs rather than on quality care can present a medical and financial nightmare to enrollees who must fight not only their illness but also bureaucratic indifference to their plight.

In our struggle to alter the crisis course of our current health care system, we must make sure that we do not rush blindly toward another system that may lead to a catastrophe of different or greater proportions.

When consumers hear about "managed care plans," they typically think of an HMO (health maintenance organization). It is important to keep in mind that there are many different breeds of managed care plans, some more restrictive than others. As in every other case discussed in previous chapters, consumer education is the key defense against exploitation and disappointment. Following are factors that should be considered when deciding whether to switch to an HMO.

What to Do When Deciding Whether to Enroll in a Managed Care Plan

- When determining whether a managed care plan is right for you, be sure to learn what type of plan you are considering and what other types of managed care plans are available in your area.

- Be aware of the types of HMOs that may be available to you as a Medicare beneficiary. Managed care plans have three different types of agreements with Medicare. The type of plan will often not be apparent from the name, but it is very important to ask what type of plan the HMO you are considering is, since this will affect your coverage. The three types of HMO plans available to Medicare beneficiaries are:

1. **Risk Contract HMOs:** Most HMOs that have arrangements with Medicare are risk contract HMOs. These plans receive a set fee from Medicare in exchange for providing all covered care. Once the member is enrolled in the plan, he or she is "locked into" receiving covered services only from the plan (except for emergency or urgently needed care).

2. Cost Contract HMOs: There are some Medicare HMOs that have cost contracts with Medicare. Under these arrangements, the enrollee may go outside the plan for services and Medicare will pay a share of the approved charges.

3. HCPP (Health Care Prepayment Plans) agreements: These plans provide services in the same general manner as a cost contract plan but often do not offer the full range of Medicare benefits. These plans can reject applicants based on preexisting health conditions and do not have to have open enrollment periods.

In addition to these three types of plans, a trial plan is being tested by Medicare in fifteen states. This additional option, called "Medicare SELECT" plans, works much like standard Medigap policies. In other words, insurance policies pick up the cost of some medical bills not covered by Medicare. Under the Medicare SELECT plans, services must be provided by the specific doctors and hospitals designated by the plan in order for the beneficiary to receive full benefits.

- Determine if you are eligible to enroll in a Medicare HMO. Most Medicare beneficiaries are eligible to enroll in a Medicare HMO. The only enrollment requirements are:
—You must be enrolled in Medicare Part B (which pays doctor bills) and continue to pay your Part B monthly premium. You do not need to be eligible for Part A of Medicare, which pays hospital bills.
—You must live within the area in which the HMO has agreed to provide services.
—You cannot be receiving care in a Medicare-certified hospice. But you may continue in a Medicare HMO if you become eligible for hospice care after having enrolled in the HMO.
—You cannot be medically determined to have end-stage renal dis-

ease (permanent kidney failure), although if you develop permanent kidney failure after joining an HMO, the plan will provide, pay for, or arrange for your care.

- Be aware that one type of Medicare HMO, the HCPP, does not operate in the same manner as risk or contract HMOs. HCPPs generally cover only Medicare Part B services and often have restrictions on enrollment, such as being available only to members of a particular group, or have restrictions regarding preexisting medical conditions.

- See what HMOs are available in your area. To get the names of Medicare HMOs that provide services in your area, contact your State Insurance Counseling Office (see Appendix 3, page 156) or call Medicare at 1-800-638-6833.

- Find out when you can join your chosen HMO and when your coverage is effective. Plans that contract with Medicare have an advertised open enrollment period of at least thirty days once a year. The plan must enroll Medicare beneficiaries in the order of application during these open enrollment periods.

- Be sure that you get written information from the plan explaining your coverage and when it goes into effect (plans are required to provide you with this information). You may choose to have your coverage begin either on the first day of the month after your enrollment application is received by the plan or up to three months later.

- Find out what benefits are covered by the plan. A major advantage of HMOs is that many plans offer comprehensive benefits to plan members.

- Ask whether the plan you are considering offers periodic routine physicals, regular screenings, flu shots, eye and hearing exams, dental care, prescription drugs, inpatient or outpatient mental health benefits, chiropractic care, routine foot care, care in skilled nursing facilities, home care, and ambulance services. Also ask if 100 percent of hospital costs are covered by the plan.

- If there is more than one Medicare HMO in your area, compare the benefits offered by each plan to determine which is a better situation for you considering your own particular needs.

- Find out how much the plan will cost you out-of-pocket, whether there are copayments for particular services, and what the monthly premiums are. It may be easier to anticipate costs you will have to bear out-of-pocket with an HMO, since you will know the amount of the premium in advance and there may be set copayments for certain services. In many cases, benefits that are provided beyond Medicare-covered services are available at low or no additional charges though the plan.

- Find out if you have to receive all covered care from the plan or if you can "go outside the plan" for care. This is a crucial fact to find out, since the rules differ according to the type of contract the plan has with Medicare. Getting this information is very important, since you may be responsible for the entire cost of your medical bills if you receive care outside the plan when this is not allowed.

  Risk contract HMOs have so-called "lock in" requirements, meaning that you are generally locked into receiving all covered care through the plan or through referrals by the plan. This means that, except in emergencies or cases of urgently needed care, you are responsible for the entire bill if you go to a physician or hospital outside the plan for services that have not been approved. In such cases, Medicare will not pick up any part of the bill.

Cost contracts are less restrictive and generally do not have "lock in" requirements, thus allowing you to choose between plan providers and paying only a copayment, or going outside the plan and having Medicare pay its share of the bill while you pick up deductibles and coinsurance.

- Find out if you can choose your own doctor of if one is selected for you. Most managed care plans allow you to select a primary care physician from a list of doctors affiliated with the plan, or assign you a doctor to manage your care if you do not choose one.

- If you have a trusted primary care physician or specialist, find out if he or she is a provider in the plan. This is a major consideration, especially if you do not want to give up a doctor who has been managing your care for many years. Also ask about specialists you may need.

- Learn how you can change your primary care physician if you are not pleased with your choice. Since your primary care physician is responsible for managing your care and admissions to hospitals, you should be comfortable with your choice. Ask how the plan allows you to change primary care physicians.

- If your own doctor is not on the plan's list of providers, ask your friends or plan members about the doctors on the list to get a sense of whether you would be comfortable choosing any of them as your doctor. Find out if they are accepting new patients and how long you have to wait for appointments.

- Find out what hospitals and other services the plan uses and determine whether they are conveniently located for you.

- Ask the plan about the qualifications of the doctors in the plan, how often the HMO reviews their performance, and how you can file any complaints you may have about physician services.

- Find out how soon you can get appointments for non-emergency care and whether you go directly to the doctor's own office for care or to a central location.

- Learn how the plan defines emergencies and what care is covered for you when you are out of the plan's service area. These factors are especially important to consider if you travel often, since many plans will not cover expenses for health care that might have been needed before you went outside the plan's service area on a trip. Also, you and the plan may disagree on how to define "emergency" care. Be sure you know these rules before signing up for HMO coverage.

- Think about whether you should keep your Medigap coverage while you are in a Medicare HMO. Generally, you do not need a Medigap supplemental policy while you are enrolled in a managed care plan, since you may be paying twice for the same coverage. For example, if you enroll in a risk contract HMO and go outside the plan for services, neither Medicare nor the Medigap policy will pay for benefits.

    You should be aware that while you are enrolled in a Medicare HMO, insurers are prohibited from selling you a Medigap policy, since this would duplicate your benefits in violation of federal law.

    However, if you already have a Medigap policy when you are considering an HMO, you may want to think about keeping your Medigap coverage while you decide if you like the plan. If you enroll in the HMO and later decide to leave the plan and return to traditional Medicare coverage, it may be harder for you to buy a Medigap policy on the same favorable terms. This is especially important to consider if you have medical conditions that may preclude you from purchasing a Medigap policy (or limit your coverage) after you leave the HMO.

- Ask about the rules for canceling your enrollment in the plan and whether you would be eligible for Medigap coverage if you decide to leave the HMO.

  Under Medicare rules, you may disenroll from a Medicare HMO at any time. To end your enrollment, state in writing to your plan and your local Social Security (or Railroad Retirement Board) office that you want to withdraw from the plan and return to traditional Medicare coverage. You may also change from one Medicare HMO to another approved Medicare HMO.

  Again, keep in mind that if you gave up your Medigap insurance policy while you were in the HMO, you may have to pay higher premiums or be unable to get coverage due to preexisting medical conditions.

- Find out if your enrollment can be canceled and under what circumstances.

- Find out your appeal rights and grievance procedures for problems you have with your HMO. Carefully review the membership materials provided by the plan to determine how you file an appeal.

  Medicare does provide certain rights for beneficiaries enrolled in HMOs. You can file an appeal if your plan refuses to pay for Medicare-covered services, refuses to provide services you request, or decides not to pay for the care you received from doctors or hospitals outside the plan on the grounds that they were not for emergency or urgently needed out-of-area care.

- Be sure to talk with your friends or members of the plan you are considering to see if they have been satisfied with the services the plan provides.

- Know where you can go for additional information about managed care plans, as well as other supplemental Medicare insurance coverage.

    States often have free volunteer counseling services available on the types of managed care and Medigap supplemental insurance policies that are available. Contact your state department of insurance or state or local office on aging. (State contacts are included in Appendices 2 and 3, pages 151 and 156.)

CHAPTER ELEVEN

The Russians Are Coming

Whether you like it or not, history is on our side. We will bury you.

—Nikita Khrushchev

We are going to do something terrible to you—we will deprive you of your enemy.

—Mikhail Gorbachev

For nearly forty-five years after World War II, the United States and the Soviet Union were locked in a Siberian embrace, setting each others cities and military facilities in the cross hairs of thermonuclear weapons, hurling hot, rhetorical volleys across the Atlantic and Pacific oceans, and either waging or seeking to contain wars of liberation. There was no guarantee that either an act of madness or miscalculation might not unleash tens of thousands of fire-breathing monsters that would turn our nations into radioactive ash heaps. And so, as children, we practiced protective drills that required us to avoid looking at a sudden, holocaustic flash of light, hide under our school desks, and evacuate buildings in an orderly fashion that were certain to crumble.

In retrospect, now that we understand the utter destructive power of nuclear megatonnage, these measures, along with those of our parents who were asked to store one or two months of supplies in the basements of our homes, seem mindlessly silly.

There is no need here to debate whether the United States won the Cold War (which I believe is the case) or that the Soviet Union's military reach exceeded its grasp and it simply collapsed of its own weight. We know this: The Berlin Wall is down and the Soviet empire has been dismantled. The United States and its Western allies no longer live in perpetual apprehension of an East–West confrontation that could result in the vaporization of much of life on this planet.

But the paranoic fear that the "Russians are coming" has materialized in a wholly unanticipated fashion. Accompanying the transition from a communistic, dictatorial regime to a democratic political system and a free market economy has been the release of a wave of violent crime. More than 5,600 organized criminal groups now operate in Russia. Their activities embrace the full range of illegality—drug trafficking, murder, theft, extortion, gambling, prostitution, bribery, kidnaping, fraud and even the sale of nuclear materials.

A number of powerful Russian gangs have set up operations in London, on the French Riviera—and in the United States. Although these gangs are pursuing the same activities that they pursue in Russia with equivalent levels of ruthlessness, our health care system has become one of their new and profitable targets. Recognizing that nearly $1 trillion is spent on health care in the United States each year, and that there is a severe shortage of law enforcement personnel and large loop holes in our legal system, these criminals have devised schemes to rob our medical reimbursement system blind.

The Angora Swap

One such scheme recently surfaced in New York City. A company with alleged ties to the Russian Mafia directed its telemarketing campaign toward the Russian emigré community in the Brighton Beach section of Brooklyn. The emigrés were offered angora undergarments, valued at approximately $50, in exchange for their Medicaid card numbers. Once these numbers were obtained, the company would bill Medicaid for $1.5 million for expensive medical equipment, such as orthotic back supports, that was never ordered by any physician and rarely, if ever, delivered to the emigrés.

From New York to California

In another New York case, the manager of a Brooklyn-based durable medical equipment company and partners in a telemarketing firm were convicted of stealing $1.8 million from a Medicaid program by fraudulently sending out bills for a variety of medical supplies never ordered by physicians, and for double-billing for disposable diapers for hundreds of nursing home residents. The manager was so bold as to advertise in a local Russian language newspaper that the Medicaid recipients could obtain free beds, mattresses, tables, raised toilet seats, and bathroom stools.

In Southern California, two Russian immigrant brothers allegedly masterminded an operation involving "rolling labs"—mobile laboratories that served patients at health clubs, retirement homes, shopping centers, and mobile home parks. The brothers set up boiler room telemarketing operations to solicit patients by offering them comprehensive medical examinations at free or nominal costs.

The patients would fill out a medical history form. A series of diagnostic tests would be performed and the medical forms would then be falsified to reflect medically necessary tests and services that would be reimbursable by a private insurance company or state or federal program. The brothers, whose operation had spread to St. Louis, Chicago and Florida, were charged with filing $1 billion in false claims, of which they received approximately $50 million.

In addition to draining away millions of dollars from our health care system, the perpetrators of this scheme endangered the lives of the people they purported to treat. The perfunctory nature of the examinations that were performed failed properly to diagnose the medical condition of some of the patients and gave them a false sense of security. Others were shocked to discover that their insurance companies had been notified that they were suffering from high blood pressure, heart disease, diabetes, obstructive pulmonary emphysema, or cancer.

While many of these schemes involved the use of inducements to acquire access to patients' private or governmental insurance rights, we can expect that intimidation and coercion will be employed whenever blandishments or deception prove insufficient.

"Throughout the United States, organized criminal groups have compromised doctors, chiropractors, and attorneys," says Louis Freeh, the FBI director. "These groups have established store-front clinics, diagnostic testing companies, and bogus law offices. They stage phony car accidents." The FBI director explained:

> As part of the scheme, phony patients visit the clinics, generating bills for exaggerated medical procedures that are provided. These include unnecessary tests for MRI's, X rays, and other sophisticated tests which are performed and billed to insurers. In some cases, bills are submitted when no medical treatments were even administered. The bogus law offices then collect personal injury claims. Further, these groups have extorted and physically intimidated witnesses. Their schemes have resulted in billions of dollars in losses to insurers and increased premiums to policyholders . . . ."

A recent case demonstrates the ruthless brutality of some of the thugs operating in the United States. In June 1995, the FBI arrested Vyacheslav Kirillovich Ivankov and five of his associates and charged them with conspiracy to commit extortion. Ivankov is regarded as one of the most powerful Russian crime leaders in the United States.

He had formed a criminal organization in Russia in 1980, and served ten years in prison for theft. After his release in 1991, he began to build a criminal network in the United States and gained entry here in 1993 and set up his headquarters in Brighton Beach, Brooklyn.

In November 1994, several of Ivankov's associates began to extort money from an investment advisory firm in New York City. They made multiple demands for sums ranging from $2.7 million to $5 million. They carried out a threat to kill the father of one of the partners and murdered him in Moscow. Thereafter, they kidnaped the partners, drove them to a restaurant in New Jersey, and forced them to sign an agreement to pay $3.5 million to one of Ivankov's surrogates.

It's clear that where making or taking money is the object, there are no limits known—or mercy shown—by the criminals who want it.

It's important to remember that organized criminal groups that have been feeding voraciously on our health care system are not bounded by ethnicity. Virtually every nationality has representation in the "thieves' world." Groups who once specialized in cocaine smuggling have turned to health care fraud because their chances of being apprehended and incarcerated for lengthy terms are remote.

Federal law enforcement officials have not waved a white flag in surrender to the lawless. In fact, the Justice Department has declared that the apprehension and prosecution of health care fraud is one of its top priorities, second only to violent criminal activity in importance.

The results of the FBI's shift in focus and allocation of resources have been impressive. In 1994, for example, through its enhanced efforts on health care fraud the FBI achieved 353 criminal convictions and recovered $480 million in fines, recoveries, and restitution, in addition to $32.7 million in proceeds that were seized or forfeited to the government.

Operation Gold Pill

Perhaps the most successful major investigation of health care fraud was an undercover effort, code-named "Operation Gold Pill," which spanned the years 1989 to 1993.

Federal and state law enforcement officials discovered a scheme that not only depletes health care funds of millions of dollars but endangers the lives of an unsuspecting public. Corrupt physicians and their assistants have concocted what one official has described as a "blood for pill" scheme.

Medicaid recipients who are in no need of medical attention visit a "Medicaid mill" and allow physicians' assistants to draw blood and perform numerous unnecessary tests for which the recipients receive a prescription for expensive medications which they have no intention of using. The recipients then proceed to a pharmacy— which may or may not be operating in good faith—and have the prescriptions filled.

For this facet of the scheme, the Medicaid system is double- billed: once by the clinic for the recipients' visits and the numerous unnecessary blood tests, and second by the pharmacy for the prescriptions that it has filled. The scheme does not stop at this point. Thereafter, the Medicaid recipients sell the drugs to a low-level street hustler, known as a "non-con man," for, say, ten cents on the dollar.

The non-con man sells the drugs to a higher-level diverter at a substantial discount, takes the pills from their original vial or bottle, dumps them into larger plastic bottles or bags, and then resells them at a discount to a still higher-level diverter who has more cash on hand to deal in greater volumes. He, in turn, will sell the drugs to a dishonest pharmacist at a 25 percent to 40 percent discount. The pharmacist then repackages the pills and sells them at full value to those in legitimate need of the drugs. The purchaser will either pay the costs out of pocket or, in many cases, have the costs billed to Medicaid.

This scheme not only results in the double and triple billing of the Medicaid system but also puts the ultimate consumer in danger of receiving tainted or unsafe medications—as the drugs often lack expiration dates, which disclose their potency, and the lot numbers, which are essential in the event of a recall by the manufacturer.

The FBI has found that these drugs are often stored in open and unsealed containers and are not temperature-controlled. In one case, agents seized $750,000 worth of pills that were stored en masse in a shed. The Miami heat and humidity had caused the drugs to break down, become powdery, and contaminate other medications with which they had been stored. In a similar case in New York, agents seized a large volume of antibiotics that had been stored in a roach-infested closet.

This drug diversion scheme is not the product of dim-witted thugs from Palookaville. Rather it reflects a sophisticated business network (worthy of Harvard MBA graduates) that has reached from New York to Miami to San Juan, Puerto Rico, to Los Angeles.

The FBI-led undercover operation also involved the expertise of the Food and Drug Administration and the New York Department of Professional Discipline. Pharmacists and street-level diverters got jail sentences between eight and twelve months and fines ranging up to $40,000. The higher-level diverters received jail sentences that ranged from one to three years with similar fines.

In the final stages of "Operation Gold Pill" the FBI dedicated 500 agents to break up this particular fraudulent scheme. But victory here must be tempered with the sobering reality that this one success does not a prison make for all of the criminals who prey upon our health care system.

While not every doctor or pharmacy is unscrupulous enough to engage in this type of activity, these diversions are a significant criminal problem in this country and have become a high priority for the FBI.

But being caught does not mean being punished severely. FBI telephone wiretaps reveal two diverters discussing their profits and mocking criminal penalties, saying, "Most of the time you get twenty years to life you walk out on your own recognizance."

The drug diversion operatives continue to flourish and our law enforcement officials will need greater resources and reinforcements if we are to wage an effective war against those who are ripping off our health care system.

Given the billions of dollars at stake and the strength and reach of organized crime's tentacles, many may be tempted to abandon all hope and yield to the inevitable flood tide of corruption. But we should be mindful that nothing is inevitable until it happens and that history is replete with examples of those who, at the very bleakest of moments, overcame what appeared to be impossible odds.

On the afternoon of July 2, 1863, during the Civil War battle at Little Round Top in Gettysburg, Colonel Joshua Chamberlain, a Bowdoin College professor-turned-warrior found himself facing catastrophe. His war-weary unit, the Twentieth Maine Volunteer Regiment, was running out of ammunition at a time when a forward-moving Confederate army outnumbered his men two-to-one. He knew that within a matter of minutes, his beleaguered forces would be overrun and the Union's military position at Gettysburg hopelessly compromised.

In a burst of extraordinary courage and ingenuity, he ordered his men to fix bayonets and charge down the hill. The sight of two hundred screaming men surging down from Little Round Top with the sun glinting on their steel bayonets so stunned the Confederate forces that they either surrendered or retreated in full flight. That singular act of boldness marked a major turning point in the war. It came as no surprise that Ulysses S. Grant elevated Chamberlain to the rank of general for the extraordinary leadership he demonstrated throughout the Civil War and selected him to receive the formal Confederate surrender at Appomattox.

We cannot expect this turn of history to be reenacted today. The FBI cannot charge in full-throated cry down from Washington's "shining city on a hill," and expect to frighten the organized forces that confront us. New legislation that gives federal law enforcement officials greater legal ammunition and firepower are desperately needed. "Operation Gold Pill" resulted in the felony convictions of sixty-five defendants. By all accounts it was a major success.

But the FBI learned a number of important lessons in the course of this undercover investigation. First, criminal investigations of this scope cannot be effectively completed using traditional investigative tools. Second, tremendous amounts of manpower are required to track and break up these criminal operations. It is far too time-consuming and cumbersome for investigators to rely upon mail-fraud and wire-fraud statutes to secure evidence and convictions of those engaged in criminal fraud. There is need for a separate, straightforward statute that will allow our law enforcement officials to prosecute health care fraud.

There is also need for clearer, tougher penalties against those who willfully defraud the health care system and for greater authority to be given to Medicare and other federal health care programs to kick out fraudulent doctors, equipment companies, or other health care providers who are ripping off these programs. Only when these con artists learn they can no longer do business with the government will they get the message that skimming money off of Medicare, Medicaid, or other health care programs doesn't pay. We need to keep taxpayers' money from getting into the pockets of these swindlers. And we need to impose stiff fines and penalties.

Last year, the Congress took steps to toughen the government's response to those who plunder the nation's treasury without care or concern for the well-beling of vulnerable senior citizens. Specifically, the Congress passed legislation to beef up the efforts of the government and private insurance industry to combat fraud and abuse in the health care system. The new law will:

- First, release resources devoted to health care fraud enforcement by funneling some of the monies recovered from fines, penalties, and other sanctions imposed on those convicted of health care fraud back into a fund that would pay for more health care fraud investigators and prosecutors.
- Second, subject those who commit major health care fraud to stiffer criminal penalties and prevent them from doing business with Medicare, Medicaid, or other government health care programs.
- Third, better coordinate the efforts of federal agencies that have responsibilities for enforcing health-care fraud laws.
- Fourth, subject those who commit lesser health care fraud offenses to administrative fines and penalties. Under current law, too many "small-time" health care fraud offenders get away with their crimes because the government doesn't have the time or resources to pursue criminal cases.
- Fifth, clarify the rules on what is and what is not allowed under Medicare and other government health care programs for doctors and other providers, so that honest providers will not get trapped or accused of committing fraud simply because the rules are so complicated.

Passing new laws and expanding our law enforcement capabilities, while long overdue, will prove only partially successful in defeating the scoundrels and cheats who will always be among us. In truth, we can never hire enough "white collar policemen" to walk the computerized streets of our health care system and prevent the thieves from breaking and entering our treasury vaults. Much more is required. It will be necessary for an energized citizenry to join in the effort to protect and defend a fundamental societal imperative— the care and comfort of those in need of high-quality and affordable medical treatment.

Regrettably, too many hold the mistaken belief that government agencies are capable of protecting the integrity of our health care programs. Others rationalize that as individuals we are helpless to confront a massive and indifferent bureaucracy or the machinations of a clever criminal class that lives beyond the reach of legal codes or ethical dictates. The first notion, we have seen, is a fiction, and the second, a confession of unconditional surrender.

There is no problem too large or complicated that cannot be solved by an intelligent analysis and a mobilized determination on the part of a free people. If each individual, however, concedes that "I am only one against many," or "It's not coming out of my pocket," then, of course, the baton of responsibility will be passed along a line that stretches into infinity—and to defeat. We need to adopt the stern virtues and determination displayed by Otto Twitchell and Sam Vitale (see Chapter One). As they showed, each of us has a moral responsibility to protest error or wrongdoing on the part of others. Only then we will release a collective energy that will shatter what we thought to be impenetrable barriers.

AFTERWORD

The thrust of this book is that our nation's elderly are easy prey for society's predators. This is a premise in need of qualification. It is true that the elderly are viewed as prime targets by society's miscreants. As we have seen, the elderly are likely to have liquid savings or capital assets that they have accumulated through hard work and frugal living. Having lost a spouse, they may live alone and lack the support system offered by an extended family. Some may not only be alone, but lonely for companionship, attention, and displays of affection, and therefore more vulnerable to the cunning and deceitful. And they may suffer from infirmities that limit their ability either to comprehend or resist high-pressure sales tactics that are designed to separate them from their bank accounts.

But we must take care not to overgeneralize. The elderly, in fact, are no more susceptible to the importunings, flatteries, and deceptions than any other age group. Moreover, we indulge in fundamental error in seeking to define or circumscribe what constitutes *being* elderly and *who* qualifies for membership.

In this regard, I think often of the enormous contribution made by once-senator, then-congressman Claude Pepper of Florida, the first chairman of the House of Representatives Select Committee on Aging, a committee that was abolished in 1993. Paramount among his many missions in life was Pepper's unrelenting desire to change society's perceptions of, and policies toward, our nation's elderly. He scheduled a congressional hearing to solicit testimony from active older Americans about laws requiring mandatory retirement age for employees of the federal government who had reached age 65.

At the time it was adopted, policymakers no doubt viewed the law as socially desirable and humane. After all, 65 was seen as pushing the mortality limits, and surely a person ought to enjoy a few years of surcease after so many of toil. Besides, a surplus of labor required older workers to make way for the young.

But much of that had changed. Medical science had scored break-throughs that extended the envelope of our existence. People were living longer, healthier lives and demographic realities no longer dic-tated that older workers step aside for an infinite and unbroken line of younger ones.

Chairman Pepper called many prominent and well-respected older Americans to speak on their continuing contributions to society. The distinguished witnesses included actress Ruth Gordon, then age 80; Colonel Harland Sanders, founder of the Kentucky Fried Chicken restaurant chain, then age 86; and actor Will Geer, then age 75, who portrayed "Grampa Walton" in the popular television series "The Waltons."

Geer wanted to talk about something other than demographics. He wanted to speak of spirit and heart. As he concluded an impas-sioned plea to the members of the committee, urging us to cast off the rusty chains of the past that imprisoned those who were still eager and able to work, he explained, "A man does not really seri-ously start to work from dawn until dark until he is 70 years of age."

Geer's powerful delivery brought forth a burst of approval from the audience, not unlike that one might hear as a theater's stage curtain descends upon an actor who has just delivered a magnificent final soliloquy. After the hearing was adjourned, Geer approached me, and with an inner light dancing in his eyes said, "A man has to have a podium to pound on, and when you take that podium away, you take away his reason for living and his zest for life."

Not surprisingly, the legislation to repeal the mandatory retirement law was changed. No longer must federal employees cross over into the valley of disuse when time's shadow touches 65. More than the law was changed. We altered our attitudes as well.

Governments tend to see people through the eyes of census-takers or statisticians. But people are not fungible goods like so many wheat stalks or widgets. Rather, we are individuals with unique abilities, aspirations, and ambitions. We have seen how some people are physically old and spiritually depleted at 50, while others are still young at 75.

Until October 7, 1995, when my father died at the age of 86, he continued to work eighteen hours a day, six days a week in his bakery. I should add that he did so with the assistance of my mother who devoted nearly as many hours while also running a household and maintaining a spectacular garden that remains the envy of our community.

I remember well their reaction when a press release that emanated from my office several years ago described my parents as "elderly." Both were chagrined, my father more so. Elderly to them meant that they were dependent or enfeebled, and they were neither. They were vigorous and fully engaged in productive activity. Indeed, not one of their children or grandchildren could keep their pace.

Their disappointment was a necessary reminder that we must never allow our thought process to soften and slip into convenient generalities or stereotypes when seeking to define problems or describe people.

So no, it is not that the elderly—however defined—are easy marks. What makes their victimization so damnable is not that they are weaker of body or more wounded in mind than others (although we have seen examples where such is the case), but rather that they have virtually no opportunity to recover from their financial and psychological wounds. Their bank accounts cannot be replenished or their dreams dusted off and restored. They are left then to depend upon the kindness of strangers and the mercies of friends.

Fraudulent activity permeates virtually every facet of our political system—from the purchase of food stamps, military armaments, housing projects, computer and information technology to every program designed to benefit our neediest citizens, including Medicare and Medicaid.

Societies usually decay from within. Soft vices, if long ignored, turn to moral rot which eats away at the foundations of institutions until the structure of government itself collapses. When government agencies no longer fulfill their promise or purpose, when laws are violated and programs ravaged with impunity, when individuals no longer exercise care or express concern over larcenist conduct because the thievery does not appear to touch them directly, then our noble experiment in self-government is likely to end in ruin or revolution.

Therefore, it's imperative to issue a call to bear arms, not those fashioned for weaponry, but for a citizen's army equipped with information and education. In this way, we can form an effective front line of defense against the jackals who lurk in the tall grass, always on the watch for those who go unprotected and unsuspecting.

We must do this without illusion or false hope, but mindful of Kant's ethical tutorial that perfection is not ours to possess. Even if we were capable of constructing a perfect castle to house our people and erecting an impenetrable fortress against those who bear us evil, both structures would come under assault from within and without from the very day that the last stone of the sanctuary was laid.

Democratic societies, and the institutions fashioned by human hands and minds, cannot look forward to completion, only to perpetual struggle, and that is because we will always be in the process of *becoming*.

This is not meant to be a cynical and weary-eyed assessment of the fate of humankind, but rather an exhortation to face the future that will always be filled with change and challenge and to do so with a mighty heart.

The poet Robert Browning put it more simply. Our reach must always exceed our grasp.

That's what the heavens are for.

National Hotlines

American Association
  of Retired Persons   (800)424-3410

National Association of
  Insurance Commissioners   (202)624-7790

National Coalition Against
  Domestic Violence   (202)783-5332

Social Security   (800)772-1213

Call Social Security to find out how
  and when to enroll for Medicare
  or get a new card.

Medicare hotline   (800)638-6833

State Agencies on Aging

ALABAMA
Commission on Aging
RSA Plaza, Suite 470
770 Washington Avenue
Montgomery, Alabama 36130
(205)242-5743

ALASKA
Division of Senior Services
Department off Administration
3601 C Street #380
Anchorage, Alaska 99503
(907)563-5654

ARIZONA
Aging and Adult Administration
Arkansas Department of Human
  Services
P.O. Box 1437, Slot 1412
7th and Main Streets
Little Rock, Arkansas 72201
(501)682-2441

CALIFORNIA
Department of Aging
1600 K Street
Sacramento, California 95814
(916)322-5290

COLORADO
Division of Aging and Adult
  Services
Department of Social Services
110 16th Street, 2nd Floor
Denver, Colorado 80203-1/14
(303)620-4127

CONNECTICUT
Director of Community Services
Department of Social Services
Elderly Services Division
25 Sigourney Street, 10th Floor
Hartford, Connecticut 06106-5033
(203)424-5281

DELAWARE
Division of Services for Aging and
   Adults with Physical Disabilities
Department of Health and Social
   Services
1901 North DuPont Highway
New Castle, Delaware 19720
(302)577-4791

DISTRICT OF COLUMBIA
Office on Aging
One Judiciary Square
441 4th Street NW, 9th Floor
Washington, DC 20001
(2020724-5622

FLORIDA
Department of Elder Affairs
Building B, Suite 152
4040 Esplanade Way
Tallahassee, Florida 32399-7000
(904)414-2000

GEORGIA
Office of Aging
#2 Peachtree Street NE, 18th Floor
Atlanta, Georgia 30303
(404)657-5258

HAWAII
Executive Office on Aging
Office of the Governor
335 Merchant Street, Room 241
Honolulu, Hawaii 96813
(808)586-0100

IDAHO
Office on Aging
Room 108-Statehouse
Boise, Idaho 83720
(208)334-3833

ILLINOIS
Department on Aging
421 East Capitol Avenue

Springfield, Illinois 62701
(217)785-2870

INDIANA
Bureau of Aging/In Home Services
402 W. Washington Street
   #E-431
Indianapolis, Indiana 46207-7083
(317)232-7020

IOWA
Department of Elder Affairs
Jewett Building, Suite 236
913 Grand Avenue
Des Moines, Iowa 50309
(515)281-5187

KANSAS
Department of Aging
Docking State Office Building, 122-
   S
915 S.W. Harrison
Topeka, Kansas 66612-1500
(913)296-4986

KENTUCKY
Division of Aging Services
Cabinet for Human Resources
275 East Main Street, 6 West
Frankfort, Kentucky 40621
(502)564-6930

LOUISIANA
Office of Elderly Affairs
P.o. Box 80374
4550 N. Boulevard, 2nd Floor
Baton Rouge, Louisiana 70806
(504)925-1700

MAINE
Bureau of Elder and Adult Services
Department of Human Services
State House, Station #11
Augusta, Maine 04333
(207)624-5335

MARYLAND
Office on Aging
State Office Building, Room 1004
301 West Preston Street
Baltimore, Maryland 21201
(410)225-1100

MASSACHUSETTS
Executive Office of Elder Affairs
1 Ashburton Place, 5th Floor
Boston, Massachusetts 02108
(617)727-7750

MICHIGAN
Office of Services to the Aging
P.O. Box 30026
Lansing, Michigan 48909
(517)373-8230

MINNESOTA
Board on Aging
444 Lafayette Road
St. Paul, Minnesota 55155-3843
(612)296-2770

MISSISSIPPI
Council on Aging
Division of Aging and Adult
  Services
750 N. State Street
Jackson, Mississippi 39202
(601)359-4929

MISSOURI
Division of Aging
Department of Social Services
P.O. Box 133
615 Howerton Court
Jefferson City, Missouri 65102-133
(314)751-3082

MONTANA
Governor's Office on Aging
State Capitol Building
Capitol Station, Room 219

Helena, Montana 59620
(406)444-3111

NEBRASKA
Department on Aging
P.O. Box 95044
301 Centennial Mall-South
Lincoln, Nebraska 68509
(401)471-2306

NEVADA
Division of Aging SErvices
Department of Human Resources
State Mail Room Complex
Las Vegas, Nevada 89158
(702)486-3545

NEW HAMPSHIRE
Division of Elderly and Adult
  Services
State Office Part South
115 Pleasant Street Annex
  Building #1
Concord, New Hampshire 03301-
  3843
(603)271-4680

NEW JERSEY
Division on Aging
Department of Community Affairs
CN 807
South Broad and Front Streets
Trenton, NJ 08625-0807
(609)984-6693

NEW MEXICO
State Agency on Aging
La Villa Riviera Building
224 East Palace Avenue, 4th Floor
Santa Fe, New Mexico 87501
(505)827-7640

NEW YORK
Office for the Aging
New York State Plaza

Agency Building #2
Albany, New York 12223
(518)474-44225

NORTH CAROLINA
Division of Aging
CB Palmer Drive
Raleigh, North Carolina 27626-
0531
(919)733-3983

NORTH DAKOTA
Aging Services Division
Department of Human Services
P.O. Box 7070 Northbrook Shop
Center
North Washington Street
Bismark, North Dakota 58507-
7070
(701)328-2577

OHIO
Department of Aging
50 West Broad Street, 9th Floor
Columbus, Ohio 43266-0501
(614)466-5500

OKLAHOMA
Oklahoma Aging Services Division
Department of Human Services
P.O. Box 25352
312 N.E. 28th Street
Oklahoma City, Oklahoma 73125
(405)521-2327

OREGON
Senior and Disabled Services
Division
600 Summer Street, NE, 2nd Floor
Salem, Oregon 97310-1015
(503)945-58111

PENNSYLVANIA
Department of Aging
MSS Office Building

400 Market Street, 7th Floor
Harrisburg, Pennsylvania
17101-2301
(717)783-1550

RHODE ISLAND
Department of Elderly Affairs
160 Pine Street
Providence, Rhode Island 02903-
3708
South Carolina
Division on Aging
Office of the Governor
202 Arbor Lake Drive #301
Columbia, South Carolina 29223
(803)737-7500

SOUTH DAKOTA
Office of Adult Services and Aging
700 Governors Drive
Pierre, South Dakota 57501
(605)773-3656

TENNESSEE
Department on Aging
P.O. Box 12786 Capitol Station
1949 Highway 35 South
Austin, Texas 78741-3702
(512)444-2727

UTAH
Division of Aging and Adult
Services
Department of Social Services
Box 45500
120 North-200 West
Salt Lake City, Utah
84145-0500
(801)538-3910

VERMONT
Aging and Disabilities
103 South Main Street
Waterbury, Vermont 05676
(802)241-2400

VIRGINIA
Department for the Aging
700 Centre, 10th Floor
700 East Franklin Street
Richmond, Virginia 2319-2327
(804)225-2271

WASHINGTON
Aging and Adult Services
  Administration
Department of Social and Health
  Services
P.O. Box 45050
Olympia, Washington
  96504-5050
(206)586-3768

WEST VIRGINIA
Office of Aging
Department of Health and Human
  Resources
Holly Grove - State Capitol
Charleston, West Virginia 25305
(304)558-3317

WISCONSIN
Bureau of Aging
Division of Community Services
217 S. Hamilton Street,
  Suite 300
Madison, Wisconsin 53707
(608)266-2536

WYOMING
Commission on Aging
Hathaway Building, Room 139
Cheyenne, Wyoming 82002-0710
(307)777-7986

APPENDIX THREE

Health Insurance Counseling Programs

Every sate has a free health insurance counseling program that can give information and assistance with Medicare, Medicaid, Medigap, long-term care and other health insurance benefits. The following 800 numbers work only within the state. Call them for help or advice.

State and phone number:

Alabama (800)243-5463
Alaska(800)478-6065
Arizona (800)432-4040
Arkansas (800)852-5494
California (800)927-4357
Colorado (303)894-7499
Connecticut(800)443-9946
Delaware (800)336-9500
District of Columbia

(202)676-3900
Florida (904)922-2073
Georgia(800)669-8387
Hawaii(808)586-0100
Idaho(800)247-4422
Illinois(800)548-9034
Indiana(800)452-4800
Iowa(515)281-5705
Kansas(800)432-3535

Kentucky(800)372-2973
Louisiana(800)259-5301
Maine(800)750-5353
Maryland(800)243-3425
Massachusetts(800)882-2003
Michigan(517)373-8230
 (800)882-2003
Mississippi (800948-3090
Missouri (800)390-3330
Montana(800)3322272
Nebraska(402)471-4506
Nevada(800)307-4444
New Hampshire (604)271-4642
New Jersey(800)792-8820
New Mexico(800)792-8820
New York(800)333-4114
North Carolina(800)443-9354
North Dakota(800)247-0560

Ohio(800)686-1578
Oklahoma(405)521-6628
Oregon(800)722-4134
Pennsylvania(717)783-8975
Puerto Rico(809)721-5710
Rhode Island(800)322-2880
South Carolina(800)868-9095
South Dakota(605)773-3656
Tennessee(800)525-2816
Texas(800)252-3439
Utah(801)538-3910
Vermont(800)642-5119
Virginia(800)552-3402
Washington(800)397-4422
West Virginia (304)558-3317
Wisconsin(800)242-1060
Wyoming(800)438-5768

Medicare Part B Carriers

Part B carriers can answer questions about medical insurance (part B).

Note: In many cases, the toll-free 800 numbers listed below work only within the sate. If you are calling from outside the state, use the long distance commercial number. These numbers are for the use of beneficiaries and should not be used by doctors and suppliers.

ALABAMA
Medicare/Blue Cross-Blue Shield of
  Alabama
P.O. Box 830140
Birmingham, Alabama 35283-0140
(800)292-8855
(205)988-2244

ALASKA
Medicare/Aetna Life Insurance
  Company
200 S.W. Market Street
P.O. Box 1998

Portland, Oregon 97207
(800)452-0125 (Alaska to Oregon
  customer service site)
(503)322-6831
  (customer service site in Oregon)

ARIZONA
Medicare/Aetna Life Insurance
  Company
P.O. Box 37200
Phoenix, Arizona 85069
(800)352-0411
(602)861-1968

ARKANSAS
Medicare/Arkansas Blue Cross and
Blue Shield
P.O. Box 1418
Little Rock, Arkansas
72203-1418
(800)482-5525
(501)378-2320

CALIFORNIA
Counties of Los Angeles, Orange,
San Diego, Ventura, Imperial,
San Luis Obispo, Santa Barbara:
Medicare/Transamerica Occidental
Life Insurance Company
Box 30540
Los Angeles, California
90030-0540
(800)675-2266
(213)748-2311
Rest of State: Medicare Claims
Department
Blue Shield of California
Chico, California 95976
(In are codes 209, 408, 415, 510,
707, 916, (800)952-8627
(916)743-1583
(In these area codes-213, 310, 619,
714, 805, 818, 909)
(800)848-7713
(714)796-9393

COLORADO
Medicare/Blue Shield of North
Dakota
Governor's Center II
600 Grant St., Suite 600
Denver, Colorado 80203
(800)247-2267
(701)282-0691

CONNECTICUT
Medicare/The Travelers Companies
538 Preston Avenue
P.O. Box 9000

Meriden, Connecticut
06454-9000
(800)982-6819
In Hartford: (203)72806783
In the Meriden Area:
(203)237-8592
DELAWARE
Xact Medicare Services
P.O. Box 890065
Camp Hill, Pennsylvania 17089-
0065
(800)851-3535

DISTRICT OF COLUMBIA
Xact Medicare Services
P.O. Box 890065
Camp Hill, Pennsylvania 17089-
0065
(800)233-1124

FLORIDA
Medicare/Blue Cross and Blue
Shield of Florida, Inc.
P.O. Box 2360
Jacksonville, Florida 32231
Copies of Explanation of Your
Medicare Part B Benefits notices,
requests for MEDPARD directo-
ries, brief claims inquiries (status
or verification of receipt), and
address changes:
(800)666-7586
(904)355-8899
For all you other Medicare needs:
(800)333-7586
(904)355-3680

GEORGIA
Medicare/Aetna Life Insurance
Company
P.O. Box 3018
Savannah, Georgia 31402-3018
(800727-0827
(912)9202412

HAWAII
Medicare/Aetna Life Insurance Co.
P.O. Box 3947
Honolulu, Hawaii 96812
(800)272-5242
(808)524-1240

IDAHO
CIGNA Medicare
3150 N. Lakeharbor, Lane, Suite
254
P.O. Box 8048
Boise, Idaho 83707-6219
(800)627-2782
(208)342-7763

ILLINOIS
Medicare Claims/Health Care
Service Corporation
P.O. Box 4422
Marion, Illinois 62959
(800)642-6930
(312)938-8000
TDD: (800)535-6152
INDIANA
Medicare Part B/AdminaStar
Federal
P.O. Box 7073
Indianapolis, Indiana 46207
(800)622-4792
(317)842-4151

IOWA
Medicare/IASD Health Services
Corporation
(d/b/a Blue Cross and Blue Shield
of Iowa)
Correspondence:
P.O. Box 9269
Des Moines, Iowa 50360
(800)532-1285
(515)245-4785

KANSAS
The counties of Johnson and

Wyandotte:
Medicare/Blue Cross and Blue
Shield of Kansas, Inc.
P.O. Box 419840
Kansas City, Missouri 64141-6840
(800)892-5900
(816)561-0900
Rest of state: Medicare/Blue Cross
and Blue Shield of Kansas, Inc.
1133 S.W. Topeka Boulevard
P.O. Box 239
(800432-3531
(913)232-3773

KENTUCKY
AdminaStar of Kentucky
P.O. Box 37630
Louisville, Kentucky 40233-7630
(800)999-7608
(502)425-6759

LOUISIANA
Arkansas Blue Cross and Blue
Shield, Inc.
Medicare Administration
P.O. Box 83830
Baton Rouge, Louisiana
70884-1494
(800)462-9666
In New Orleans: (504)529-1494
In Baton Rouge: (504)927-3490

MAINE
Medicare/C and S Administrative
Services
P.O. Box 1000
Hingham, Massachusetts 02044-
9193
(800)492-0919
(207)828-4300

MARYLAND
Counties of Montgomery, Prince
Georges:
Medicare Xact Medicare Services

P.O. Box 890065
Camp Hill, Pennsylvania
   17089-0065
(800)233-1124
Rest of state: Trail Blazer
   Enterprises
P.O. Box 5678
Timonium, Maryland
   21094-5678
(800)492-4795

MASSACHUSETTS
Medicare/C and S Administrative
   Services
P.O. Box 1000
Hingham, Massachusetts 02044-
   9191
For non-assigned claims:
   P.O. Box 2222
   Hingham, Massachusetts
   02044-9193
(800)882-1228
(617)741-3300

MICHIGAN
HCSC
Michigan Medicare Claims
P.O. Box 5544
Marion, Illinois 62959
(313)225-8200
(800)482-4045

MINNESOTA
Counties of Anoka, Dakota,
   Fillmore, Goodhue, Hennepin,
   Houston Olmstead, Ramsey,
   Wabasha, Washington, Winona:
Medicare/The Travelers Insurance
   Company
8120 Penn Avenue South
Bloomington, Minnesota 55431
(800)352-2762
(612)884-7171
Rest of state: Medicare/Blue Cross
   and Blue Shield of Minnesota

P.O. Box 64357
St. Paul, Minnesota 55164
(800)392-0343
(612)456-0372

MISSISSIPPI
Medicare/The Travelers Insurance
   Company
P.O. Box 22545
Jackson, Mississippi
   39225-2545
(800)682-5417
(601)956-0372

MISSOURI
Counties of Andrew, Atchison,
   Bates, Benton, Buchanan,
   Caldwell, Carroll, Cass, Clay,
   Clinton, Daviess, DeKalb,
   Gentry, Grundy, Harrison,
   Henry, Holt, Jackson, Johnson,
   Lafayette, Livingston, Mercer,
   Nodaway, Pettis, Platte, Ray, St.
   Clair, Saline, Vernon, Worth:
Medicare/Blue Cross and Blue
   Shield of Kansas, Inc.
P.O. Box 419840
Kansas City, Missouri
   64141-6840
(800)892-5900
(816)561-0900
Rest of state: Medicare General
   American Life Insurance
   Company
P.O. Box 505
St. Louis, Missouri 63166
(800)392-3070
(314)843-8880

MONTANA
Medicare/Blue Cross and Blue
   Shield of Montana, Inc.
2501 Beltview
P.O. Box 4310
Helena, Montana 59604

(800)332-6146
(406)444-8350

NEBRASKA
The carrier for Nebraska s Blue
  Cross and Blue Shield of Kansas,
  Inc. Claims, however, should be
  sent to: Medicare Part B
Blue Cross Blue Shield of Nebraska
P.O. Box 3106
Omaha, Nebraska 68103-0106
(800)633-1113

NEVADA
Medicare/Aetna Life Insurance
  Company
P.O. Box 37230
Phoenix, Arizona 85069
(800)528-0311
(602)861-1968

NEW HAMPSHIRE
Medicare/C and S Administrative
  Services
P.O. Box 1000
Hingham, Massachusetts
  02044-9191
For non-assigned claims:
P.O. Box 2222
Hingham, Massachusetts
  02044-9193
(800)447-1142
(207)828-1300

NEW JERSEY
Xact Medicare SErvices
P.O. Box 890065
Camp Hill, Pennsylvania
  17089-0065
(800)462-9306

NEW MEXICO
Medicare/Aetna Life Insurance
  Company
P.O. Box 25500

Oklahoma City, Oklahoma
  73125-0500
(800)423-2925
In Albuquerque: (505)821-3350

NEW YORK
Counties of Bronx, Columbia,
  Delaware, Dutchess, Greene,
  Ings, Nassau, New York,
  Orange, Putnam, Richmond,
  Rockland, Suffolk, Sullivan,
  Ulster, Westchester:
Medicare B/Empire Blue Cross and
  Blue Shield
P.O. Box 2280
Peekskill, New York 10566

NORTH CAROLINA
Connecticut General Life Insurance
  Company
P.O. Box 671
Nashville, Tennessee 37202
(800)672-3071
(919)665-0348

NORTH DAKOTA
Medicare/Blue Shield of North
  Dakota
711 2nd Avenue, N.
Fargo, North Dakota 58102
(800)247-2267
(701)277-2363

OHIO
Medicare/Nationwide Mutual
  Insurance Company
P.O. Box 57
Columbus, Ohio 43216
(800)282-0530
(614)249-7157

OKLAHOMA
Medicare/Aetna Life Insurance
  Company
701 N.W. 63rd Street

Oklahoma City, Oklahoma
  73116-7693
(800)522-9079
(405)848-7711

OREGON
Medicare/Aetna Life Insurance
  Company
200 S.W. Market Street
P.O. Box 1997
Portland, Oregon 97207-1997
(800)452-0125
(503)222-6831

PENNSYLVANIA
Xact Medicare Services
P.O. Box 890065
Camp Hill, Pennsylvania
  17089-0065
(800)382-1274

RHODE ISLAND
Medicare/Blue Cross and Blue
  Shield of Rhode Island
Inquiry Department
444 Westminster Street
Providence, Rhode Island
  02903-3279
(800)662-5170
(401)861-2273

SOUTH CAROLINA
Plametto Government Benefits
  Administrators
Medicare Part B Operations
P.O. Box 100190
Columbia, South Carolina 29202
(800)868-2522
(803)788-3882

SOUTH DAKOTA
Medicare Part B/Blue Shield of
  North Dakota
711 2nd Avenue, N.
Fargo, North Dakota 58102

(800)437-4762

TENNESSEE
CIGNA Medicare
P.O. Box 1465
Nashville, Tennessee 37202
(800)342-8900
(615)244-5650

TEXAS
Medicare/Blue Cross and Blue
  Shield of Texas, Inc.
P.O. Box 660031
Dallas, Texas 75266-0031
(800)442-2620
(214)235-3433

UTAH
Medicare/Blue Shield of Utah
P.O. Box 30269
Salt Lake City, Utah 84120-0269
(800)426-3477
(801)481-6196

VERMONT
Medicare/C and S Administrative
  Services
P.O. Box 1000
Hingham, Massachusetts
  02044-9191
For on-assigned claims:
  P.O. Box 2222
Hingham, Massachusetts
  02044-9193
(800) 447-1142
(207)828-4300

VIRGINIA
Counties of Arlington, Fairfax,
  cities of Alexandria, Falls
  Church, Fairfax:
Xact Medicare Services
P.O. Box 890065
Camp Hill, Pennsylvania
  17089-0065

(800)233-1124
Rest of state: Medicare/The
  Travelers Insurance Company
P.O. Box 2643
Richmond, Virginia
  23251-6463
(800)552-3423
(804)330-4786

WASHINGTON
Aetna Life Insurance Company
Medicare Part B
P.O. Box 91099
Seattle, Washington
  98111-9199
(800)37106604
In Seattle: (206)621-0359

WEST VIRGINIA
Medicare/Nationwide Mutual
  Insurance Corporation
P.O. Box 57
Columbus, Ohio 43216
(800)848-0106
(614)249-7157

WISCONSIN
Medicare/WPS
Box 1787
Madison, Wisconsin 53701
(800)944-0051
In Madison: (608)221-3330
TDD (800)828-2837

WYOMING
Blue Cross and Blue Shield of
  North Dakota
P.O. Box 628
Cheyenne, Wyoming 82003
(800)442-2371
(307)632-9381

State Insurance Consumer Services Departments

ALABAMA
Insurance Department
Consumer Services Division
135 South Union Street
P.O. Box 303351
Montgomery, Alabama
   36130-3351

ALASKA
Division of Insurance
800 East Dimond, Suite 560
Anchorage, Alaska 99515
(907)349-1230

ARIZONA
Insurance Department
Consumer Affairs Division
2910 North 44th Street
Phoenix, Arizona 85018
(602)912-8444

ARKANSAS
Insurance Division

Seniors Insurance Network
1123 South University Avenue
Suite 400
Little Rock, Arkansas 72204
(800)852-5494

CALIFORNIA
Insurance Department
Consumer Services Division
300 South Spring Street
Los Angeles, California 90013
(213)897-8921

COLORADO
Insurance Division
1560 Broadway,
Suite 850
Denver, Colorado 80202
(303)894-7499 x356

CONNECTICUT
Insurance Department
P.O. Box 816

Hartford, Connecticut 06142-0816
(203)297-3800

DELAWARE
Insurance Department
Rodney Building
841 Silver Lake Boulevard
Dover, Delaware 19904
(302)739-4251
(800)282-8611

DISTRICT OF COLUMBIA
Insurance Department
Consumer and Professional Services
   Bureau
441 4th Street NW
Suite 850 North
Washington, DC 20001
(202)727-8000

FLORIDA
Department of Insurance
200 E. Gaines Street
Tallahassee, Florida 32399-0300
(904)922-3100

GEORGIA
Insurance Department
2 Martin L. King, Jr., Drive
716 West Tower
Atlanta, Georgia 30334
(404)656-2056

HAWAII
Department of Commerce and
   Consumer Affairs
Insurance Division
P.O. Box 3614
Honolulu, Hawaii 96811
(808)586-2790

IDAHO
Insurance Department
SHIBA Program
700 W. State Street, 3rd Floor

Boise, Idaho 83720-0043
(208)334-4350

ILLINOIS
Insurance Department
320 W. Washington Street,
   4th Floor
Springfield, Illinois 62767

INDIANA
Insurance Department
311 W. Washington Street,
   Suite 300
Indianapolis, Indiana 46204
(800)622-4461
(317)232-2395

IOWA
Insurance Division
Lucas State office Building
E. 12th and Grand Streets,
   6th Floor
Des Moines, Iowa 50319
(515)281-5705

KANSAS
Insurance Department
420 S.W. 9th Street
Topeka, Kansas 66612
(913)296-3071
(800)432-2484

KENTUCKY
Insurance Department
215 w. Main Street
P.O. Box 517
Frankfort, Kentucky 4062
(502)564-3630

LOUISIANA
Senior Health Insurance
   Information Program
Insurance Department
P.O. Box 94214
Baton Rouge, Louisiana

70804-9214
(504)342-5301
(800)259-5301

MAINE
Bureau of Insurance
Consumer Division
State House, Station 34
Augusta, Maine 04333
(207)582-8707

MARYLAND
Insurance Administration
Complaints and Investigation Unit-
   Life and Health
501 St. Paul Place
Baltimore, Maryland 21202-2272
(410)333-2793
(410)333-2770

MASSACHUSETTS
Insurance Division
Consumer Services Section
470 Atlantic Avenue
Boston, Massachusetts 02210-2223
(617)521-7777

MICHIGAN
Insurance Bureau
P.O. Box 30220
Lansing, Michigan 48909

MINNESOTA
Insurance Department
Department of Commerce
133 E. 7th Street
St. Paul, Minnesota 55101-2362
(612)296-4026

MISSISSIPPI
Insurance Department
Consumer Assistance Division
P.O. Box 79
Jackson, Mississippi 39205
(601)359-3569

MISSOURI
Department of Insurance
Consumer Services Section
P.O. Box 690
Jefferson City, Missouri 65102-
   0690
(800)726-7390
(314)751-2640

MONTANA
Insurance Department
126 N. Sanders
Mitchell Building, Room 270
P.O. Box 4009
Helena, Montana 59601
(406)444-2040

NEBRASKA
Insurance Department
Terminal Building
941 O Street, suite 400
Lincoln, Nebraska 68508
(402)471-2201

NEVADA
Department of Business and
   Industry
Division of Insurance
1665 Hot springs Road,
   Suite 152
Carson City,Nevada 89710
(702)687-4270
(800)992-0900

NEW HAMPSHIRE
Insurance Department
Life and Health Division
169 Manchester Street
Concord, New Hampshire 03301
(603)271-2261
(800)852-3416

NEW JERSEY
Insurance Department
20 West State Street

Roebling Building
CH 325
Trenton, New Jersey 08625
(609)292-5363

NEW MEXICO
Insurance Department
P.O. Drawer 1269
Santa Fe, New Mexico
   87504-1269
(505)827-4500

NEW YORK
Insurance Department
160 West Broadway
New York, New York 10013
(212)602-0203
(800)342-3736 (outside NY)

NORTH CAROLINA
Insurance Department
Seniors' Health Insurance
   Information Program
P.O. Box 26387
Raleigh, North Carolina 27611
(919)733-0111 (SHIIP)
(800)662-7777 (Consumer
   Services)

NORTH DAKOTA
Insurance Department
Senior Health Insurance Counseling
600 E. Boulevard
Bismark, North Dakota
   58505-0320
(800)247-0560
(701)328-2440

OHIO
Insurance Department
Consumer Services Division
2100 Stella Court
Columbus, Ohio 43215-1067
(800)686-1526
(614)644-2673

OKLAHOMA
Insurance Department
P.O. Box 53408
Oklahoma City, Oklahoma
73152-3408
(405)521-6628

OREGON
Department of Consumer and
   Business Services
Senior Health Insurance Benefits
   Assistance
470 Labor and Industries Building
Salem, Oregon 97310
(503)378-4484
(800)722-4134

PENNSYLVANIA
Insurance Department
Consumer Services Bureau
1321 Strawberry Square
Harrisburg, Pennsylvania 17120
(717)787-2317

RHODE ISLAND
Insurance Division
   233 Richmond Street,
Suite 233
Providence, Rhode Island
   02903-4233
(401)277-2223

SOUTH CAROLINA
Department of Insurance
Consumer Services Section
P.O. Box 100105
Columbia, South Carolina
   29202-3105
(803)737-6180
(800)768-3467

SOUTH DAKOTA
Insurance Department
500 E. Capitol Avenue
Pierre, South Dakota

57501-5070
(605)773-3563

TENNESSEE
Department of Commerce and
   Insurance
Insurance Assistance Office,
   4th Floor
500 James Robertson Parkway
Nashville, Tennessee 37243
(800)525-2816
(615)741-4955

TEXAS
Department of Insurance
Complaints Resolution, MC 111-
   1A
333 Guadalupe Street
P.O. Box 149091
Austin, Texas 78714-9091
(512)463-6500
(800)252-3439

UTAH
Insurance Department
Consumer Services
3110 State Office Building
Salt Lake City, Utah
   84114-6901
(800)429-3805
(801)538-3805

VERMONT
Department of Banking and
   Insurance
Consumer complaint Division
89 Main Street, Drawer 20
Montpelier, Vermont
   05620-3101
(802)828-3302

VIRGINIA
Bureau of Insurance
Consumer Services Division
1300 Main Street

P.O. Box 1157
Richmond, virginia 23209
(804)371-9741
(800)552-7945
WASHINGTON
Insurance Department
4224 6th Avenue SE, Building 4
P.O. Box 40256
Lacey, Washington 98504-0256
(800)562-6900
(360)753-7300

WEST VIRGINIA
Insurance Department
Consumer Services Division
2019 Washington Street East
P.O. Box 50540
Charleston, West Virginia 25305-
   0540
(304)558-3386
(800)642-9004
(800)435-7381 (hearing impaired)

WISCONSIN
Insurance Department
Complaints Department
P.O. Box 7873
Madison, Wisconsin 53707
(800)236-8517
(608)266-0103

WYOMING
Insurance Department
Herschler Building
122 W. 25th Street
Cheyenne, wyoming 82002
(800)438-5768
(307)777-7401

Nursing Home Checklist

Following is a list of some things to look for when deciding on a nursing home. After your initial visit, make one or two unannounced visits and mealtimes or on weekends to confirm you findings.

What to look for:

❏ Home has arrangements with a nearby hospital to transfer residents in case of emergency.

❏ Home has arrangements with a nearby pharmacy to deliver medications, though you may use a different pharmacy if you prefer.

❏ The residents appear well groomed, are dressed in street clothes, and are involved in activities.

❏ Floors, bedding, and furniture are clean and in good repair.

❏ No strong body or urine odors throughout building.

- ❏   No strong chemical deodorants used throughout building.

- ❏   Food looks appetizing and healthy.

- ❏   Staff and administrators are accommodating in allowing you to look around, ask questions, and talk with the residents.

- ❏   The staff speaks to residents as adults, not children.

- ❏   All charges are disclosed up front: Request a written list of extra charges.

- ❏   Home will keep patients when they apply for Medicaid.

- ❏   Laundry is handled regularly and efficiently.

- ❏   Residents can eat in their rooms if they prefer.

North American Securities Administrators

ALABAMA
Securities Commission
770 Washington Street
Suite 570
Montgomery, Alabama 36130-
    4700
(205)242-2984
(205)265-4033 fax

ALASKA
Department of Commerce &
    Economic Development
Division of Banking, Securities, &
    Corporations
State Office Building, 9th Floor
333 Willoughby Ave.
P.O. Box 110807
(907)465-2521
(907)465-2549 fax

ARIZONA
Corporation Commission

Securities Division
1300 West Washington
Third Floor
Phoenix, Arizona 85007
(602)542-4242
(602)542-3583 fax

ARKANSAS
Securities Department
Heritage West Building
201 East markham, Third Floor
Little Rock, Arkansas 72201
(501)324-9260
(501)324-9268 fax

CALIFORNIA
Department of Corporations
3700 Wilshire Boulevard,
    Suite 600
Los Angeles, California 90010
(213)736-2741
(213)736-3593 fax

COLORADO
Division of Securities
1580 Lincoln, Suite 420
Denver, Colorado 80203
(303)894-2320
(303)861-2126 fax

CONNECTICUT
Department of Banking
260 Constitution Plaza
Hartford, Connecticut 06103
(203)240-8299
(203)240-8178 fax

DELAWARE
Department of Justice
Division of Securities
State Office Building
820 N.French Street, 8th Floor
Wilmington, Delaware 19801
(302)577-2515
(302)655-0576 fax

DISTRICT OF COLUMBIA
Securities Commission
450 5th Street, N.W., Suite 821
Washington, D.C. 20001
(202)626-5105
(202)737-2080 fax

FLORIDA
Office of Comptroller
State of Florida
Department of Banking & Finance
Plaza Level, The Capitol
Tallahassee, Florida 32399-0350
(904)488-9805
(904)681-2428 fax

GEORGIA
Office of the Secretary of State
Securities & Business Regulation
    Division
Two Martin Luther King, Jr., Drive
802 West Tower

Atlanta, Georgia 30334
(404)656-2894
(404)657-8410 fax

HAWAII
Department of Commerce &
    Consumer Affairs
1010 Richards Street
Honolulu, Hawaii 96813
Mailing Address: P.O. Box 40
    Honolulu, Hawaii 96810
(808)586-2744
(808)586-2733 fax

IDAHO
Department of Finance
Securities Bureau
700 West State Street
Boise, Idaho 83720
Mailing Address: P.O. Box 83720
Boise, Idaho 83720-0031
(208)334-3684
(208)334-3564 fax

ILLINOIS
Office of the Secretary of State
Securities Department
900 South Spring Street
Springfield, Illinois 62704
(217)782-2256

INDIANA
Office of the Secretary of State
Securities Division
302 West Washington,
    Room E-111
Indianapolis, Indiana 46204
(317)232-6681
(317)233-3675 fax

IOWA
Insurance Division
Securities Bureau
Lucas State Office Building
Des Moines, Iowa 50319

(515)281-4441
(515)281-6467 fax

KANSAS
Office of the Securities
    Commissioner
618 South Kansas Avenue,
    2nd Floor
Topeka, Kansas 66603-3804
(913)296-3307a
(913)296-6872 fax

KENTUCKY
Department of Financial Institutions
477 Versailles Road
Frankfort, kentucky 40601
(502)573-3390
(502)573-8787 fax

LOUISIANA
Securities Commission
Energy Centre
1100 Poydras Street, suite 2250
New orleans, Louisiana 70163
(504)568-5515

MAINE
Department of Professional &
    Financial Regulation
Bureau of Banking
Securities Division
State House Station 121
Augusta, Maine 04333
(207)582-8760

MARYLAND
Office of the Attorney General
Division of Securities
200 Saint Paul Place, 20th Floor
Baltimore, Maryland 21202-2020
(410)576-6360
(410)576-6532 fax

MASSACHUSETTS
Secretary of the Commonwealth

Securities Division
One Ashburton Place,
    Room 1701
Boston, Massachusetts 02108
(617)727-3548
(617)248-0177 fax

MICHIGAN
Department of Commerce
Corporation & Securities Bureau
6546 Mercantile Way
Lansing, Michigan 48910
(517)334-6213
(517)334-6155 fax

MINNESOTA
Department of commerce
133 East Seventh Street
St. Paul, Minnesota 55101
(612)296-4026
(612)296-4328 fax

MISSISSIPPI
Office of the Secretary of State
Securities Division
202 North Congress Street, Suite
    601
Jackson, Mississippi 39201
Mailing Address:
    P.O. Box 136
    Jackson, Mississippi 39205
(601)359-6364
(601)359-2894 fax

MISSOURI
Office of the Secretary of State
600 West Main Street
Jefferson City, Missouri 65101
(314)751-4136
(314)526-3124 fax

MONTANA
Office of the State Auditor
Securities Department
126 North Sanders, Room 270

Helena, Montana 59604
Mailing Address:
    P.O. Box 4009
    Helena, Montana 59604
(406)444-2040
(406)444-5558 fax

NEBRASKA
Department of Banking & Finance
Bureau of Securities
1200 N Street, Suite 311
Mailing Address:
    P.O. Box 95006
    Lincoln Nebraska 68509-
    5006
(402)471-3445

NEVADA
Office of the Secretary of State
    Securities Division
555 E. Washington Avenue,
    5th Floor
Las Vegas, Nevada 89101
(702)486-2440
(702)486-2452 fax

NEW HAMPSHIRE
Bureau of Securities Regulation
Department of State
State House, Room 204
Concord, new Hampshire 03301-
    4989
(603)271-1463
(603)224-1427 fax

NEW JERSEY
Department of Law & Public Safety
Bureau of Securities
153 Halsey Street, 6th Floor
Newark, New Jersey 07102
Mailing Address:
    P.O. Box 47029
    Newark, New Jersey 07101
(201)504-3600
(201)504-3639

NEW MEXICO
Regulation & Licensing
    Department
Securities Division
725 St. Michaels Drive
Santa Fe, new Mexico 87501
(505)827-7140 general
    information
(505)984-0617 fax

NEW YORK
Department of Law
Bureau of Investor Protection &
    Securities
120 Broadway, 23rd Floor
New York, New York 10271
(212)416-8200
(212)416-8816 fax

NORTH CAROLINA
Department of the Secretary
    of State
Securities Division
300 North Salisbury, Suite 301
Raleigh, North Carolina
    27603-5900
(919)733-3924
(919)821-0818 fax

NORTH DAKOTA
Office of the securities
    Commissioner
State Capitol,
    5th Floor
600 East Boulevard
Bismark, North Dakota 58505
(701)328-2910
(701)255-3113 fax

OHIO
Division of Securities
77 South High Street
Columbus, Ohio 43215
(614)644-7381
(614)466-3316

OKLAHOMA
Department of Securities
Journal Record Building
621 N Robinson, Suite 400
Oklahoma City, Oklahoma 73102
(405)235-0230
(405)235-0579 fax

OREGON
Department of Consumer and
  Business Services
Division of Finance & Corporate
  Securities
Labor & Industries Building
Salem, Oregon 97310
(503)378-4387
(503)378-4178 fax

PENNSYLVANIA
Securities Commission
Eastgate Office building
1010 North 7th Street,
  2nd Floor
Harrisburg, Pennsylvania 17102-
  1410
(717)787-8061
(717)783-5122 fax

PUERTO RICO
Commissioner of Financial
  Institutions
Centro Europa Building
1492 Ponce de Leon Avenue,
  Suite 600
San Juan, Puerto Rico 00909-1492
(809)723-3131
(809)723-3857 fax

RHODE ISLAND
Department of Business Regulation
233 Richmond Street, Suite 232
Providence, Rhode Island 02903-
  4232
(401)277-3048
(401)273-5202 fax

SOUTH CAROLINA
Department of State
Securities Division
P.O. Box 11350
Columbia, South Carolina 29211
(803)734-1087
(803)252-5524 fax

SOUTH DAKOTA
Division of Securities
118 West Capitol Avenue
Pierre, South Dakota
  57501-2017
(605)773-4823
(605)773-5953 fax

TENNESSEE
Department of Commerce &
  Insurance
Volunteer Plaza, Suite 680
500 James Robertson Parkway
Nashville, Tennessee
  37243-0485
(615)741-2947
(615)532-8375 fax

UTAH
Department of commerce
Division of Securities
Heber M. Wells Building
160 East 300 South
Salt Lake City, Utah 84111
Mailing Address:
  P.O. Box 45808
  Salt Lake City, Utah 84145-
  0808
(801)530-6600
(801)530-6980 fax

VERMONT
Department of Banking, Insurance
  & Securities
Securities Division
89 Main Street, Drawer 20
Montpelier, Vermont 05620-3101

(802)828-3420
(802)828-2896 fax

VIRGINIA
State Corporation Commission
Division of securities & Retail
    Franchising
1300 East Main Street,
    9th Floor
Richmond, Virginia 23219
Mailing Address:
    P.O. Box 1197
    Richmond, Virginia 23209
(804)371-9051
(804)371-9911 fax

WASHINGTON
Department of Financial
    Institutions
Securities Division
General Administration Building
210 11th St., SW,
    Third Floor West
Olympia, Washington 98504
Mailing Address:
    P.O. Box 9033
    Olympia, Washington 98507-
    9033
(360)902-8760
(360)586-5068 fax

WEST VIRGINIA
State Auditor's Office
Securities Division
State Capitol Building
1900 Kanawha Blvd. East, Room
    W-118
Charleston, West Virginia 25305
(304)558-2257
(304)344-2299 fax

WISCONSIN
Office of the Commissioner of
    Securities
101 East Wilson Street, 4th Floor
Madison, Wisconsin 53702
Mailing Address:
    P.O. Box 1768
    Madison Wisconsin
    53701-1768
(608)266-3431
(608)256-1259 fax

WYOMING
Secretary of State
Securities Division
State Capitol, Room 109
Cheyenne, Wyoming 82002
(307)777-7370

Office of the Attorney General

ALABAMA
Office of the Attorney General
State House
11 south Union Street
Montgomery, Alabama 36130
(205)242-7334
(205)242-2433 fax

ALASKA
Office of the Attorney General
1031 West 4th Avenue
Anchorage, Alaska 99501-1994
(907)269-5206
(907)278-3458 fax

ARIZONA
Office of the Attorney General
1275 West Washington Street
Phoenix, Arizona 85007
(602)542-3702
(602)542-4377 fax

ARKANSAS
Office of the Attorney General
200 Tower building
323 Center Street
Little Rock, Arkansas
72201-2610
(501)682-7506
(501)682-8084 fax

CALIFORNIA
State Office of Consumer Protection
Office of the Attorney General
P.O. Box 944255
Sacramento, California
94244-9555
(619)645-2089
(619)645-2062 fax

COLORADO
Office of the Attorney General
Department of Law

1525 Sherman Street
Denver, Colorado 80203
(303)866-5230
(303)866-5691 fax

CONNECTICUT
Office of the Attorney General
110 Sherman Street
Hartford, Connecticut 06105
(203)566-5374
(203)523-5536 fax

DELAWARE
Office of the Attorney General
Carvel State Office Building
820 North French Street,
8th Floor
Wilmington, Delaware 19801
(302)577-2500
(302)577-3360 fax

DISTRICT OF COLUMBIA
Office of the Corporation Counsel
441 4th Street NW
Washington, DC 20001
(202)727-3500
(202)727-6546 fax

FLORIDA
Department of Legal Affairs
Office of the Attorney General
4000 Hollywood Boulevard
Suite 505 South
Hollywood, Florida 33021
(305)985-4780
(305)985-4496 fax

GEORGIA
Governor's office of Consumer
    Affairs
Two Martin Luther King, Jr., Drive
Plaza Level, East Tower
Atlanta, Georgia 30334
(404)656-1762
(404)651-9018 fax

HAWAII
828 Fort Street Mall
Suite 600B
Honolulu, Hawaii 96813
(808)586-2636
(808)586-2640 fax

IDAHO
Office of the Attorney General
Statehouse
Boise, Idaho 83720-1000
(208)334-2424
(208)334-2830 fax

ILLINOIS
Office of the Attorney General
State of Illinois Center
100 West Randolph Street,
    12th Floor
Chicago, Illinois 606001
(312)814-4714
(312)814-2549 fax

INDIANA
Office of the Attorney General
Indiana Government Center South,
    5th Floor
402 West Washington Street
Indianapolis, Indiana 46204
(317)232-6205
(317)233-4393 fax

IOWA
Office of the Attorney General
Hoover State Office Building
Second Floor
Des Moines, Iowa 50319
(515)281-5926
(515)281-6771 fax

KANSAS
Office of the Attorney General
Judicial Building
301 West Tenth Street
Room 20 F

Topeka, Kansas 66612-1597
(913)296-2215
(913)296-6296 fax

KENTUCKY
Office of the Attorney General
P.O. Box 2000
Frankfort, Kentucky 40602
(502)573-2200
(502)573-8317 fax

LOUISIANA
Office of the Attorney General
Department of Justice
P.O. Box 94095
Baton Rouge, Louisiana
    70804-4095
(504)342-9638
(504)342-7901 fax

MAINE
Office of the Attorney General
State House Building, Station 6
Augusta, Maine 40333
(207)626-8800
(207)626-8828 fax

MARYLAND
Office of the Attorney General
200 Saint Paul Place
16th Floor
Baltimore, Maryland
    21202-2202
(410)576-6557
(410)576-6566 fax

MASSACHUSETTS
Office of the Attorney General
One Ashburton Place
Boston, Massachusetts
    02108-1698
(617)727-2200
(617)727-5765 fax
MICHIGAN
Office of the Attorney General

P.O. Box 30212
525 West Ottawa Street
Lansing, Michigan 48909-0212
(517)335-0855
(517)335-1935 fax

MINNESOTA
Office of the Attorney General
NCL Tower
445 Minnesota Street
14th Floor
St. Paul, Minnesota 55101-2128
(612)296-2306
(612)296-9663 fax

MISSISSIPPI
Office of the Attorney General
Consumer Protection Division
P.O. Box 22947
Jackson, Mississippi 39205
(601)354-6018
(601)354-6295 fax

MISSOURI
Office of the Attorney General
Penntower Office Center
3100 Broadway, Suite 609
Kansas City, Missouri 64111
(816)889-5000
(816)889-5006 fax

MONTANA
Department of commerce
1424 9th Avenue
Helena, Montana 59620-0501
(406)444-3553
(406)444-2903 fax

NEBRASKA
Office of the Attorney General
State Capitol
P.O. Box 98920, Suite 2115
Lincoln, Nebraska 68509-8920
(402)471-2682
(402)471-3297 fax

NEVADA
Office of the Attorney General
316 Bridger Avenue, Suite 200
Las Vegas, Nevada 89102
(702)486-3777
(702)486-3768 fax

NEW HAMPSHIRE
Office of the Attorney General
State House Annex
25 Capitol Street
Concord, New Hampshire
    03301-6397
(603)271-3658
(603)271-2110 fax

NEW JERSEY
Department of Law & Public Safety
124 Halsey Street
P.O. Box 45027
Newark, New Jersey 07101
(201)504-6534
(201)648-3538 fax

NEW MEXICO
Office of the Attorney General
P.O. Drawer 1508
Santa Fe, New Mexico
    87504-1508
(505)827-6060
(505)827-6685 fax

NEW YORK
Office of the Attorney General
120 Broadway
New York, New York 10271
(212)416-8300
(212)416-6003 fax

NORTH CAROLINA
Office of the Attorney General
Department of Justice
P.O. Box 629
Raleigh, North Carolina
    27602-0629

NORTH DAKOTA
Office of the Attorney General
State Capitol
600 East Boulevard Avenue
Bismarck, North Dakota
    58505-0040
(701)224-3404
(701)224-3535 fax

OHIO
Office of the Attorney General
State Office Tower
30 East Broad Street
25th Floor
Columbus, Ohio 43266-0410
(614)466-1306
(614)466-8898 fax

OKLAHOMA
Office of the Attorney General
4545 North Lincoln Boulevard
Suite 260
Oklahoma City, Oklahoma 73105
(405)521-4274
(405)528-1867 fax

OREGON
Financial Fraud Section
Office of the Attorney General
Justice Building
1162 Court Street NE, Suite 100
Salem, oregon 97310
(503)378-4732
(503)378-7467 fax

PENNSYLVANIA
Office of the Attorney General
Strawberry Square
16th Floor
Harrisburg, Pennsylvania 17120
(717)787-9707
(717)787-1190 fax

RHODE ISLAND
Office of the Attorney General

72 Pine Street
Providence, Rhode Island 02903
(401)274-4400
(401)277-1331 fax
South Carolina
Office of the Attorney General
Rebert C. Dennis Office Building
P.O. Box 11549
Columbia, South Carolina 29211-
    1549
(803)734-3970
(803)253-6283 fax

SOUTH DAKOTA
Office of the Attorney General
500 East Capitol
Pierre, South Dakota 57501-5070
(605)773-4400
(605)773-4106 fax

TENNESSEE
Office of the Attorney General
450 James Robertson Parkway
Nashville, Tennessee 37243
(615)741-1671
(615)532-2910 fax

TEXAS
Office of the Attorney General
Capitol Station
P.O. Box 12548
Austin, Texas 78711-2548
(512)463-2185
(512)320-0975 fax

VERMONT
Office of the Attorney General
109 State Street
Montpelier, Vermont
    05609-1001
(802)828-3171
(802)828-2154 fax

VIRGINIA
Office of the Attorney General
Supreme Court Building
101 North 8th Street,
5th Floor
Richmond, Virginia 23219
(804)786-2116
(804)371-2087 fax

WASHINGTON
Office of the Attorney General
900 4th Avenue
Suite 2000
Seattle, Washington
    98164-1012
(206)464-6733
(206)587-5636 fax

WEST VIRGINIA
Office of the Attorney General
812 Quarrier Street
6th Floor
Charleston, West Virginia 25301-
    2617
(304)558-8986
(304)558-0184 fax

WISCONSIN
Wisconsin Department of Justice
P.O. Box 7857
123 West Washington Avenue
Madison, Wisconsin
    53707-7857
(608)267-8901
(608)267-2778 fax

WYOMING
Office of the Attorney General
State Capitol Building
Cheyenne, Wyoming 82002
(307)777-7841
(307)777-6869 fax

Typical Script Used by Con-men

Hello (customer). This is (your name) with _____.
How are you today? The reason for my call is you were contacted
recently about the Award and you sent in your registration fee, that's
where the cash was to be awarded. Do you recall?

Well, anyway, the promotion is active and the major awards are
being registered and going out. It does state quite clearly here that
you are to receive one of the top awards. **SO CONGRATULA-
TIONS!!!!**

Go grab a pen and paper, _____, I'll hold on. Got it?
My name is _____ and my Company is _____.
Please make a note of the awards involved.

O.K.!!! The top Cash Award is $5,000. If awarded to you, it will be
coming to you in the form of a cashier's check. Do you use a middle

name? And the correct spelling of your last name is
_____. Is that correct? Okay. That's the top cash
award.

The Second Award is a **10K Sapphire and Diamond Bracelet,** all genuine. That's the top jewelry award.

Number three is our top Appliance Award which is a **25" Panasonic
Color Television.** Everything is state-of-the-art!

Number four is a complete **Audio Home Entertainment System,** the
whole nine yards. **Top of the line!!!**

Number five, the last award, is **$2,500.00,** also in the form of a
cashier's check.

Because you were chosen for this promotion, **you are guaranteed** to
receive one of those five. How's that sound? Now, what the company wants from you (customer) is a picture of yourself with your
major award and the right to print that in our advertisements, similar to those you've seen with Ed McMahon. Follow me? In other
words, if you were to receive one of the cashier's checks, it may
appear in our annual advertisement.

And on the bottom of our advertisement will be a perforated entry
form, inviting people to fill it out and send it in for next year's promotion. See, what we're doing is building a mailing list for the next
year. Follow me?

Okay. Let me back up a little bit. You know when any promotion is
getting started through the sales department, the reason they have
these promotions is to generate business. The salesmen usually do
tell you a few of the major awards, like the $5,000 and maybe a car

or something. Then they stick in a smaller gift, like a microwave oven or a cordless phone. That's what the majority of people wind up with obviously. Well, because the promotion is active, there are no smaller gifts. **There's just the Major Awards. . . .**

Now, (customer), I want you to understand that I need your picture with the major award you receive. You're not camera shy. Are you (customer)?

Okay. Good. Second of all, we do need an invoice to show that these major awards went to an active customer and not someone's friend or relative in the firm here. . . . So we simply send you a variety pack of our most popular gift items. The Executive Gift Pack. Your cost on that will be just $649.50 and that's all. Can you handle that comfortably? Right along with your order will be your major award, within about 21 working days. And like I said, your picture may be placed on a single page advertisement and would only appear in respectable magazines like COSMOPOLITAN, VOGUE, PEOPLE and magazines of that caliber. Is that acceptable to you? GOOD!! Take down my address. Make sure you write this down because of the timing and paperwork, I'm going to tell you exactly how we work this for you.

(GO TO DROPS PUT ON HOLD IF CAN'T AFFORD)!!!

I'm going to have my secretary call you back to help you arrange for one of these overnight couriers, probably Federal Express, to be out of there within the next two hours. You'll be there, right? Make your check payable to _____. Again, the amount is only $649.50 and that's all. Put your check in an envelope. Please make sure you put it to my attention because I'm going to handle this personally. Oh, and this is probably the most important thing, write this number down _____. Read it back to me please (wait).

GREAT!! That's your insurance number. It has to go on your check in the memo line. You see, your check comes back to the office tomorrow morning, my secretary will enter everything into the company's system and then I will insure the award for you. Sometime in the next couple of days someone in the shipping department will give you a call. We don't want any mistakes. You need to allow us about 21 working days until you receive everything. It will be delivered pre-paid. All you have to do is sign for it.

You've got my number right? (Wait, if not, give the number again.)

Promise me something, will you? When you see what you'll be receiving I want you to pick up that phone and call me so I can hear the smile on your face. FAIR ENOUGH?

And of course, if you ever need anything, please call. Okay?

Now, all I need at this time is your final authorization to register the award in your name and process everything for shipment. DO I HAVE THAT? (If yes) FANTASTIC AND CONGRATULATIONS!! (Wait) THANK YOU (go to button up)(if not, go to rebuttals and/or drop)

BUTTON UP/POST CLOSE

Now, (customer). You should like a nice person, and you're obviously able to make a good business decision, but . . . you know, I speak to a few nice people every year in regards to the major awards, and believe it or not, some people take such a liking to me that, rather than hurt my feelings, they say yes, when they really mean no. Before I go through two hours of paper work, because I really don't need the practice, if there's one chance in a thousand that you're not going to send the check, don't be nice to me. Tell me right now.

INDEX